Sacred A...

Gordon MacLellan

Sacred Animals

©1997 Gordon MacLellan

ISBN 1 898307 69 5

Cover design by Paul Mason
Cover illustration by Luke Andrew
Back cover photograph by Jamus Wood

Published by:

Capall Bann Publishing
Freshfields
Chieveley
Berks
RG20 8TF

Dedication

This book is for Ogg, a
small gorilla with a huge spirit,
and for all the toads
who have hopped through my life over the years
thank you

Thanks go to Park Records for permission to use the lyrics
from Maddy Prior's "The Fabled Hare"

Thanks also to all the hardy souls who have tried ideas
with me during "Let the Animals Dance" and other
workshops.

Contents

iv

1

Hop, Crawl, Slither, Fly and Swim

This is a book about animals. Not always animals to see or touch or run away from, but usually animals to see with the eyes of your mind, to encounter in the Other-world. Animals to wonder over in the Otherworld and in this, the physical, world. The heart of this book is the tale of a spirit journey into contact and friendship with the animal world. It is not my story - it will be yours. An adventure to start and shape and grow into fruition through connections with the spirits of the animals.

I am Pagan and I write this book from a Pagan perspective: seeing a world that is all alive, where the energy that call "life" and "spirit" moves through all things, animate, inanimate, "living" or "dead". A Pagan world is one of endless connection and communication between the individual and the inter-related, growing, changing always evolving world that that person lives in.

It is also a world of many "worlds" where one can shift perceptions to experience the everyday physical world that we are all familiar with, or to meet the spirit worlds where the life-forces of the other occupants of the physical world have their speaking awareness - worlds of stone, of water, of wind and storm and the space between the stars. From its simplest state, a pagan world can suddenly unravel itself into endless unfolding complexity as one world leads to another and another and we start to experience a universe that is so varied, such a kaleidescope of diversity, that we want to leap into it at once and sail away into the worlds we meet through our minds...

And of course, for you that may be all a lot of rubbish. This is not a problem: we all have the right to live in the reality that calls most strongly to our spirits. I would hope that this book and the activities it contains would have something to offer people of all manner of persuasions. I will write it as a pagan - you can read it as you will and translate my terms to suit your own way of looking at things. So my world of spirits and energies external to myself might become your world of archetypes contained within your subconscious.

My relationships with spirits may give you a chance to step aside from human concerns and explore your human activities from a different set of perspectives. My totems may be your guiding angels. I would hope that however you read and use *Sacred Animals* it offers you a new strength to look at and relate to the world around us and heightens the respect with which we should see and support the rest of that living, vibrant world that we are all part of.

Life is wonderful. To be alive is a wonder. To be a conscious part of the endless, spreading web of connections that links everything together is a celebration. For me "magic" is working within that awareness, with a knowledge of being a part of all that is, touching threads that also weave into all that has been and reach, unravelling, into what might yet be. That web may be the energy and dynamics of physics or the remorseless wave of evolution, it may be Wyrd, the Old Gods or the Hand of God. Whatever it is, to work in it, with it and for it makes all of life a ceremony and a celebration. If that is not "sacred", I do not know what is.

Living in the wonder of this world has its problems and it can be very easy to become so drawn into the problems that we forget that life may be just about living and that perhaps celebrating the life around us, relating to it and fitting ourselves into some sort of harmony with it might offer its own solution to those issues that beset us. Out of all the spirit world that runs through life with us, the spirits of animals are, in many ways, most similar to our own.

Most of us can relate to at least some members of the animal world, even if others may send us screaming onto a chair and that gives us some sort of a starting point for reaching out to a wider, non-human set of relationships. Animals call out responses in people. The same can, of course, also be said about trees, flowers and heavy snowfalls but they will have to wait against another occasion. *Sacred Animals* is about animals.

Those responses we make to animals are very varied. Coloured by preconceived ideas, brought up in a society that ascribes human desires and emotions to animals, we are very good at seeing them as small furry humans.

It does tend to be the furry ones: the "aaah" factor is a strong one and it is taking a lot of work to win public sympathy over to the cause of snakes, fish, bats or beetles. But it is happening, people are becoming much more aware of ecological issues and the importance of the interconnectedness of things - we need it all, even the wasps.

In *Sacred Animals* we set out to fashion personal relationships with animal spirits, to reach out beyond the physical world and beyond our interpretations of "what animals think or do" to what the spirits of those animals themselves have to say. Spirits may be those of individual animals or they represent groups of animals or even the collective awareness of a whole species.

To start with it may all feel a bit strange, or just downright silly and it is very hard to know what is "real" and what is "just imagination". There are no easy answers here. Initially, a lot of what we experience now is shaped by past experience and you will find that the spirits you may meet behave very like the animals of your childhood stories or films. This does not necessarily mean that this is all "just imagination": spirits will talk to you through the imagery you offer them and if that is all you have to work on, that is all the language they will use.

As time goes on, as you and the spirits become more used to each other and to working together, the shapes of your experiences will change as you move deeper into the spirits' world and into their perceptions of the worlds we live in.

"What is "real"? The trite answer is "whatever you want to be", which does not help a lot. The test and its proving lies inside you. When you have reached out and made contact you know it, you know the touch of an awareness that is not your own upon your life and nothing is ever quite the same again. Working with animals is one way of dropping some of those barriers we build around our human-centred world. We realise that there are other presences in this world, other beings who look at and act

4

upon the world we live in, whose awareness, needs and perceptions may be very different from our own; who put us in perspective, in our place.

In **Correspondences**, we look at the preconceptions we carry with us into this work - what animals are nice, which nasty, fast, slow, brave, cowardly and so on. Or perhaps, which ones we already associate with particular spiritual or mythical attributes. It is worth saying now that Sacred Animals tries to work without using such preconceptions.

This journey is one of discovery, the chance to learn what the animals themselves may have to teach us, not to reinforce the image systems of any particular mythos. You may be used to thinking of lions as symbols of fire, bravery and majesty, wolves as thinkers and teachers, salmon as old and wise. But really, we can learn as much about bravery from a mouse, elegance from pigeons and wisdom from beetles as anything else. Set out on this adventure with a sense of discovery and try to leave your preconceptions as far behind you as you can.

One term might need clarifying right at the start. "The Otherworld" is a collective name for that diversity of worlds not perceived with our everyday senses. For our purposes here, think of "the physical world" as being our everyday one, the world that most of us are used to working with, experienced through our five senses and which we are generally familiar with. (Of course the physical world that most of the animals you may encounter will be very different from yours, but let's not get too complicated).

"The Otherworld" is the world where you will "see" and meet with the spirits. You may enter it by going inwards, by opening the inner doors of your mind and imagination

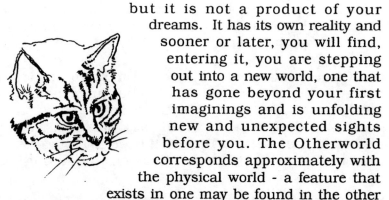

but it is not a product of your dreams. It has its own reality and sooner or later, you will find, entering it, you are stepping out into a new world, one that has gone beyond your first imaginings and is unfolding new and unexpected sights before you. The Otherworld corresponds approximately with the physical world - a feature that exists in one may be found in the other but it is not a fixed world and it changes all the time, much more quickly in some ways and slower in others than the world we are used to.

You might call it "my imagination" if that makes you more comfortable, or maybe "dream" and see the different forms of the Otherworld that you meet as the dreams of different beings. Dreams will return in deeper forms later. Me, I will call it the Otherworld, and know that for me it is also the Spiritworld, where bounds of physical size, shape, species and habitat are no longer barriers to communication.

Using this book

I work within a system that tends to rely more on intuition and instinct in planning than on carefully structured and rigidly pursued patterns of learning and development. Consequently, this book does not present a necessarily ordered study sequence.

Working with spirits is very like developing friendships - you cannot plan it all or you may stifle the growth of the relationship, while at the same time you need to walk carefully and not rush ahead, assume too much and damage things with your presumption.

You can, however, sort your intentions out into some sort of order, and there are definitely some things that you really ought to do before attempting others. Rather than definite lessons, think of these as cycles, paths that you may move along and as you move find that the spiral path you follow has become a different one and opens up to the next step in the adventure, a step that has taken you onto a different cycle.

Think too of movement on spirals as movement in two directions - an inward path that may lead from the world around you into your heart - a path of self-discovery, and another that runs from the cente of the spiral outwards, from your heart out into the world, a path of involvement in your physical and spiritual environments. With the activities in Sacred Animals, you should find that you are moving in both directions at once: in exploring the worlds around you, you find new understandings of who you are and in reaching into yourelf, you find a greater awareness of the world.

Sacred Animals is divided into three cycles:

> first cycle: identification - meeting for the first time, holding onto mages, developing contact

> second cycle: connection - exploring friendships, working with power objects

> third cycle: transformation - deeper levels of connection with masks, and dance work, fusion with the totem

Finally, there is the circle that makes the pattern complete, that supports and is supported by the other work. The circle is action - inspired by and involved with animals as spirits you carry that awareness over into your everyday life and work with or for the animals and the world that we share.

To some extent, try to follow this as a set of stages. The first and second cycles will overlap a lot and you will find yourself stepping over the hazy edge of the third cycle in some activities from the second. Do not push it, have patience and trust in the growing bonds between yourself and spirit and honesty in your own development to guide you into deeper waters when you are all ready.The circle is always there, ready for you to work with wherever you feel you are on the other cycles.

Overall, do not plan too much, or predict, do not command or control. Accept the unexpected and step out on this journey. Celebrate the lives we share - a rainbow profusion of spirits in a myriad of bodies.

Talking to the Earth

I may as well apologise in advance. *Sacred Animals* is essentially a practical book: a collection of exercises and activities for you to experiment with. While these should stand on their own several feet, the earlier book *"Talking to the Earth"* contains a lot of other activities that could prove useful. *"Talking"* is a set of environmental art activities where the underlying theme is the exploration of the world around us and the expression of our understanding of and feelings for this world through various art techniques.

Rather than repeating all those activities, there will be irritating occasions in this book where readers are referred to "*Talking*" for other ideas. Those activities are not, however, essential to the journey that we will pursue in *Sacred Animals*. They might supplement activities or offer alternatives but *SacredAnimals* should stand alone.

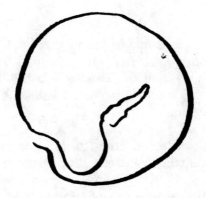

2

Stillness

Many of the exercises suggested in this book, start with an assumption about stillness. The ability to relax and slip, however, briefly, out of the hustle and bustle of everyday life is a basic magical and personal skill and will be called on again and again.

Of course, that almost inevitably means that this is something much easier written about than done.

With the growing awareness of the value of meditation in all its various forms, many people have now met and perhaps developed their own routes to that relaxed and tranquil state where contemplative work can begin. There are many way of doing this and many books and classes that may help you perfect your own path to stillness and explain for those who want it the intricacies of the changing states of your mind. In the absence of these strategies, a couple of ideas follow along with concepts about sacred spaces that may be of use in using the activities in this book.

Learn to be still. Trick that busy,busy; don't stop; always something to do; must worry about this; must plan that, front of your consciousness into letting go of its bid for total mind control long enough for the rest of you to open up - for the graceful, flowing depth and the laughing, listening awareness of you to surface. Learn to stop.

The knack is not to confront all that buzzing cloud of conscious thought but to sidestep it and, if anything, let it go like a handful of balloon strings and as the balloons go sailing, babbling, away, to enjoy the open hand that is then revealed.

In the beginning, start somewhere quiet and comfortable - with practice you should be able to relax into a meditative state in noisier places but keep it as easy as possible to begin with. So: somewhere quiet, maybe put on some gentle music, have a chair to sit in, or a cushion to sit on, or a floor to lie on. Be at ease, but not so easy that you fall asleep. I usually work cross-legged on a floor cushion or against a wall or a tree for a bit of support.

Oh, just sit down.
Now, breathe.
Gently.
In - and out.
Perhaps add a count...
In for 3, and out for 3.
In and out.

In - feel it fill your lungs and the rest of your body respond to the intake. With each inhalation, feel your body from the inside and be aware of your tensions.

And breathe out. And each exhalation allows you to release a little more tension. Feel shoulders settle, knots along your spine uncurling, furrowed brows smooth.

Keep going.

In.

And out.

Let go.

Be at your ease.

I usually give this a set of about 10 cycles of "In...and out", breathing comfortably, not very deeply, or lightly, but whatever feels acceptable. By "10" be mellow. There are probably lots of little thoughts buzzing around but you should find there is some relaxed distance from them, as if you are watching them flying around outside a window.

There will be irruptions of sudden thoughts - jobs to do, worries to worry over, ideas for dinner. It begins to feel, at times, like a competition between your conscious intellect and the rest of your awareness. Try not to confront these thoughts: to face them may mean switching on all your other thought processes again: we are trying to remain relaxed and contemplative.

I find it more effective to know that I am away from my everyday business, moving in the Otherworld of dream and shadow. Sure enough like a cloud of occasional mosquitoes "everyday business" will come rushing in. Let it come, and go. If they will not pass on, breathe those mosquitoes away: use another "in and out" to take hold of them and dissolve them.

The whole process is one of those frustrating balancing acts and at first you feel as if it is completely hopeless and will never work. But give it time. Try a couple of different techniques until you find one that helps you slip into stillness. Persevere and do not try too hard.

As you find your stillness, find also, in yourself, a relaxed person, a gentled person. Your breath will slow and

As this experience forms around you, reach out to one part of it all and concentrate gently upon it and make of it a thing to feel in detail, to touch. Use the colour and fineness of it. Something you could hold in your hands is useful here as you can pick it up with the fingers of your imagination, turn it over, feel it, recite the words that describe it.

Learn to be able to move from a general experience and atmosphere - my moor, wood, and pool above - to a precise awareness of an object - or an experience. In this case I might pick up a piece of twisted wood lying on the moor.

A variation on the above can use the place itself to help relax further. Examples:

> **a pool:** sitting by this pool, thoughts rise as bubbles and disturb the surface. I watch from the edge and the bubbles slow and slowly stop. I become still as the pool stills and I am like the pool, cool depth with a trembling surface.

> **a stream:** another pool, the current runs over a pebbly bed but the water is cloudy. As I watch, the stream clears slowly, shifting ribbons of silt fading away until I see/feel the brightness of the water and the roundness of the stones.

> **a field of flowers and grass**, moving under ruffling breezes. The wind dies until eventually I stand in a calm sea of colour and vibrancy. I am swallowed into a mouse.

A Sacred Space

Any of the above could move on to become a more permanent personal space: a site which you can almost automatically step into as you relax. This space will grow and change as your work develops and will become your "sacred space" - a place in the Otherworld that is yours and yours alone. A safe space where you can go and work and watch, and be watched. It is yours, it is safe: nothing may enter unless you permit it.

Start, as above, with an outdoor setting of comfort and peace and return to it again and again: explore it, establish its boundaries: big enough for action but not so huge that you cannot look from one side to another. Find the features that mark these boundaries: walk them, dance them, work your own ceremonies that help strengthen and define them.

If you are of a ritual turn of mind: a ceremony performed in the physical world, if done while you are holding the picture of your sacred space in your head, will also happen there. Cleansing a circle's rim with incense smoke, blessed water and a chanted verse will all echo in your sacred space and reinforce it.

The intention is not to create a fortress against besieging enemies, but to establish a space where you can step into the Otherworld and feel safe. It will always be there for you, a place to return to after wider journeys or to rest in, to invite other spirits to join you in. Your sacred space will grow of itself as well: it will gradually settle into your local Otherworld geography. It slowly moves from being your own imaginative creation to being a part of the Otherworld's dream so that the landscape around it may change slightly, new plants may grow in it, the trees may alter shape as it settles in.

Remember the Otherworld is not fixed in the way the physical world is, but changes and flows. It can be confusing but your sacred space will be there, your own stepping stone, your portal and your refuge.

Finishing

With work deep inside your head - or maybe outside of your body - it is always important to be able to stop. If you get to the end of a session and just say "oh, that's it. Let's away", leap to your feet and go shopping, you will be lining yourself up for a lively encounter with a bus. You have been working far from the face you use in dealing with the everyday world and you need to give yourself time to slip back into "normal" drive again.

When you are ready to stop, try counting back down from 10 to 0, drawing yourself back into yourself as you count down. Say "thank you" and "fare well" to your sacred space, breathe yourself back into alertness and sharpness.

Press your hands on the ground, or the floor, as a connection to the earth below, draw on its strength, sharpen your thoughts, open your eyes. Clap sharply once to break the concentration. "Earth" yourself. Give yourself a few minutes to potter about and be vague. Make yourself a cup of tea and have a piece of toast. Write things down in a journal.

If for any reason you do need to leap into action, that is possible but there is a tendency to feel as if there are bits of yourself rushing to catch up with the rest (which they will do, given time). And give yourself a chance to rest as soon as you can after whatever crisis has passed. Do not feel that in working with stillness you are about to become an inert, lifeless lump for half an hour or so: you can always act, but treat yourself as gently as possible to get as much out of the experience as you can.

First Cycle

Identification

The journey begins with contact, introductions and getting to know one another. Keep this relaxed and gentle, a set of friendly encounters. Do not go rushing in demanding, or even expecting, spirits to come rushing out in turn to meet you, delighted at your prominent arrival.

Take it easy, enjoy the moment.

Set sail on your journey and learn to speak.

3

First Contact

Starting points are often difficult to choose. You may have an animal in mind right from the start and feel that you really must set off in search of your wildebeest, or that your personal horror of rabbits is bound to bring one hurtling straight out of the unknown and onto your lap.

Let us assume, however, that you are beginning this journey with a general interest in animal-kind and no immense preferences at the moment - or at least a readiness to avoid your own preconceptions and see who comes a'visiting.

Making those first contacts can be like sitting alone in a night-club watching everyone else spinning by while no-one seems interested in you at all. And as in that club, rather than let this become depressing, turn it around and enjoy watching the scenery. Relax, appreciate the passing activity and when you are ready step out into the stream and see what happens.

To make new contacts, there are a variety of ideas you could follow...

1. Getting Ready

To begin, we need to prepare ourselves for contact and let all our new-practised skills of stillness relax us, and simply be. First encounters may not be at all dramatic. Wait, open your awareness and meet whatever comes, however briefly. It is a sensitising process, readying both self and spirit world for contact. Like the nightclub, some people will drift in, have a look and move on, others may linger for a chat. Do not assume that the first animal you see, in flesh or spirit, is going to be yours. It may just be passing through as well.

2. Catching Images

Go and sit somewhere. Choose a park bench, perhaps, or a tree to lean against. Relax as far as you can and simply watch. You do need to relax, but if you have been working on a "sacred space" as well, draw upon this if you feel you would value the security. On the whole with these activities we are not moving so much into the Otherworld as deepening our awareness of the physical one. Start with eyes closed and gradually open your senses. Listen. Smell. Look at last. See the shapes and colours of nodding, bobbing, courting, cooing pigeons. Be still and let sparrows and chaffinches come close. See, hear, feel the heavy passing of bumblebees and observe butterfly, robin and blue tit. There are very few places in this country where you will not see a bird or an insect or fail to find a spider spinning. Look for a sweep of colour and the flurry of wings that mark the hectic arrival of starlings - or watch for the silent, secret movement of mice on underground train stations.

You are looking for images. Do not try to go all profound on a park bench (or not yet, anyway). Cherish your images

and take them home. I do this by holding onto moments:
like snapshots of the animals. Discarding ideas of good
and bad animals to work with, I try to hang onto the ones
that have most caught my attention: the ones that raised a
smile or that wrapped me up in fascination. I may quickly
do a scribbled sketch or a few words (see that chapter
later) to help hold onto the image but essentially, I would
aim to leave the place with a pictures of a couple or three
animals drifting around in my head.

3. Wilder Places

In urban areas there are animals who are relatively used
to human presence and carry on their business regardless

of our presence, or set out to get as much out of us as they can. You may choose to go somewhere less populous and see if you can encounter some of the shyer residents of the wild.

You can set about this expedition in a similar way, but some extra thought and preparation may help:

avoid bright colours and rustling clothes - be as visually inconspicuous as possible

wear something that helps break up your human outline - even a hood helps, or a hat. A cloak is usefully anonymous (and alarms passers-by!)

position yourself to break that human shape - sit against a tree or under a hedge, or if you are in the middle of a field, try wrapping yourself in a blanket like a stray boulder

avoid wearing perfumes or oils - they act like alarm bells to the more sensitive noses of wild mammals

have patience

be quiet (no personal stereos either)

don't smoke
choose your time with care - dawn and dusk are often the best - animals are more active and you are less conspicuous

if you want to see a particular type of animal, try reading up on that animal's habits and take advice on the best ways of watching it

or for invertebrates (unsects and the like) be completely obvious and spread a white sheet on the ground on a sunny day. All sorts of things may come investigating. A light trap of a dark evening works likewise, only now spread your sheet under a bright lamp in a field, woodland edge or by a pool.

When you find somewhere, stop and sit. Go into your stillness and wait. Even if you do not see any animals you may find you have had a deliciously peaceful time. Go home to try again another day.

4. Watching Ponds

Having a strong inclination toward toads, I am somewhat partial to ponds and cheerfully recommend these for initial encounters. In and around a pond or other water body, you will find a wide range of animal life and sooner or later most of the larger animals of the neighbourhood will drop in. You might choose to settle beside a pond (and curse the mosquitoes), following the guidelines above. More exciting can be to lie down beside a pond and peer into its depths. Pond-watching is a much neglected delight. Let your eyes adjust to scale and reflections and in the waters of a clear pond (when the initial fright of your shadow has passed) you will see whole pageants unfolding with enough of a range of drama, grace, savagery and courtship to satisfy most tastes.

5. Catching Images 2

If going outside is not appropriate, you could reach out for a first encounter by using pictures. In workshops, I use a set of animal postcards that I have gathered over the years - an assortment of animals, mostly to be found in Britain with a few exotics thrown in for good measure. Animal totem and other "medicine" cards could also be used here, or pictures cut out of magazines. These are spread face down inside a circle of people who reach out and take one when they feel ready.

If you use pictures, try to float the image you have chosen in the stillness of your thoughts. Glance at the card and away several times, calling up the colours in your head, the texture of its skin, its eyes as they open and look at you, the way it moves its head, the way it stirs. Use your hand to stroke the animal as if it lay in front of you, run your hand over it and give it shape. If you now stand up this can easily become a dance. Or catch four words, or eight, that describe the animal, the atmosphere it brings, your feelings in these first moments... The chapter on dance later on has more livelier activities for making first contacts without necessarily watching animals themselves.

Video images are always a possibility rather than pictures on paper or card. You would need to experiment here. I find there is a tendency, even with the sound off, to be carried away by the film-makers' dream rather than a more free association with the animal. And the chances are that you will actually have chosen the animal you want to work with in your choice of video so the more unexpected element that comes with other activities may have gone. In a mixed video, animals may be presented in sequence so unless you can fumble for the remote and "pause" the shot, you may loose the image that suddenly calls out to you. Video or television may offer the chance to fly with birds or run with wolves but if you make a spirit connection with that animal you will, somewhere along the line, meet that for yourself anyway - without the technology - when you are ready for it. Equally, moving images can offer incredibly rich visuals to absorb and dwell upon - and watching rainforest scenes or whales swimming on a huge IMAX screen is an opportunity not to be missed!

The aim in all these activities is to make contact. It may not feel as if you have done anything very profound, but here we are just knocking on the door of the spirit world and, however slight, recognise that the presence of an animal in your head as at least a readiness to go a little further. Even in these simple activities, people report feelings of excitement, a sudden contact that says "let's go!" or the peace that unfolds with bird wings.

Greet your new animal friend and walk on to explore the animal through words or fetishes, to shape your friendship with dance, mask and drama.

4

Correspondences

In most cultures we find sets of associations where a particular animal, plant or other item implies a particular activity, behaviour or other quality. These may take the form of cliches that have slipped into daily use and become ingrained in language and popular belief. Some British ones might include; "elephants never forget","the lion is the king of the beasts", "black cats are unlucky", "black cats are lucky", "sheep are stupid" and as for rabbits, well everyone knows about them! We are all used to these most basic of associations and often use them without thinking: lions are strong and noble, rats are sneaky and horrible, snakes are slimy and villainous, dogs are man's best friend and bitches are to be avoided, small furry animals are cute, insects are unpleasant, all bees and wasps sting horribly, and as for rabbits....

These are conventions and are rooted in culture, not in natural history and different cultures will have different associations for different animals. Butterflies, for example, in Gaelic folklore represent death in some circumstances while in certain Native American cultures they are a gift from the Creator Spirit to the world and animals of beauty and delight. I try to avoid accepting stereotypes like these and one of the basic principles within this book is that we learn from animals what the animals choose to bring. They carry their own value: to use animals as descriptions to insult people is an insult to the animals.

Within a faith or a magical tradition more elaborate associations are well established and used as "correspondences" where the presence of one component of a set connects the believer to all the others. Some of the most commonly used systems relate to the compass points known variously as the "Four Directions", "The Watchtowers", "The Quarters" and others. One such set might look like this:

north
bull
element: earth
colour: black
time of day: midnight
time of life: old age
time of year: winter

west
dolphin
element: water
colour: blue
time of day: evening
time of life: middle age
time of year: autumn

east
hawk
element: air
colour: yellow
time of day: evening
time of life: birth/childhood
time of year: spring

south
lion
element: fire
colour: red
time of day: noon,
time of life: adolescence/young adult
time of year: summer

Different systems associate different features with each quarter: for example, you might variously find your southern quarter occupied by a dragon, a porcupine, a turkey or an eagle.

If you work within a tradition you are usually expected to accept its correspondences, but it is important to remember that they are "just" conventions. These are patterns by which we organise our relationship with the universe. They are not fixed, immutable cosmic laws. As conventions that help you work within a group and, as a group, within a body of learning, correspondences are very valuable but do not expect the spirits that you meet to necessarily recognise or conform to them.

Within animal work, the correspondences relating to different animals are extensive and outside the remit of this book: suggestions are given in the bibliography for further study. Or explore the folklore that is associated with the belief system you are involved in, if any, to find out what animals "mean" when they appear in stories or in spells.

Within our context here, however, you might start to work with the idea of a world that can be approached from four directions, each direction offering different components that together make the vibrant whole. You might use the exercises below to start building up a personal set of correspondences so that you will have your own animal connections to different qualities and the like. Or you might turn things around and find that one animal will bring different attributes to a situation depending upon which direction it approaches you from...

Four Quarters

Working with the idea of the compass directions offering a basic division of the world, mark out those four directions on your floor, or in the grass around you. Go into your stillness, in the centre of this space, find that calm place within you and then turn to face each direction in turn.

With each quarter, face outwards and say to yourself something like:

> *"I face the east,*
> *I face the sunrise,*
> *I feel the wind on my face..."*

Starting from the obvious (sunrise), let yourself feel outwards. Reach out towards the east for a colour, a time of day, a season, weather and, somewhere, an animal who carries the feeling of "the east of the world" to you. If you find this too nebulous, you could use the cards we met in **Catching Images 2** and draw an animal card from your pack for each quarter and explore how that association feels, and what it brings.

Go on to work your way round the quarters and then come back and try "up" and "down" and "centre" as final directions.

Four Elements

You could follow the same process through using elements as starting points - these are of course the "mythic" rather than the "periodic table" elements. If you wanted to work your way from Hydrogen, through Helium and onwards, you could do so but it would take quite a while. In western traditions there are usually four elements: earth, air, fire and water, sometimes with "spirit" coming in as a fifth. Other traditions may incorporate other elements - metal, wood and more.

One Animal

Instead of working with different animals at each quarter, if you have started developing a relationship with one animal, turn things around and now ask your animal what it brings with it when it comes walking from the different directions.

Again, start with stillness, and reach out to your animal. Turn to face each direction in turn and ask your animal, "what do you bring when you come from the west of the world?"

You are unlikely to get a verbal response, more a set of rippling images: the animal with water, the animal in autumn, the animal as a watcher, or a hunter, in strength, in speed, in courtship, in labour.

The **One Animal** associations are a powerful way of building up an understanding of the qualities that this animal brings to your friendship. This helps things develop in a more organised way than might otherwise be the case.

The pattern that grows will be affected by your own previous associations with different directions but that is not necessarily a bad thing. Do try to avoid expecting the animal to approach your circle as "earth, strength and winter" from the north just because that is where you think they should be: hedgehog strength may come from a summery south and hedgehog winter might be about stillness, patience and biding time. **One Animal** will tend to be personal and may apparently conflict with established correspondences if you are working within a tradition. Remember that these associations are your own, and hold them still while doing group or other "formal" work - or invite your group to meet your new associations themselves and see how these work within an ever unfolding, rich and varied world.

5

Words

Words are our basic tools for describing - and defining - our world. We use them so casually that it is easy to forget their power. Words shape our world. We use them like walls to contain that world: what we can frame with words, delineate, define, limit, becomes "real". We use words to mark the edge of the world, and beyond the edge lies impossibility. And words can lift people up, inspire them, humiliate, enchant or destroy them. Language is magical. We do not think of it as so but our words change the world we live in all the time.

Modern story-tellers are talking again about "wonder-tales" rather than myths, legends and fairy-stories. Myths have become almost acceptedly allegorical: handy ways of exploring archetypes and stereotypes, and the kingdoms of Faerie are still struggling to escape from being "fairies". But "wonder-tales" are just that: stories told for the delight and the enchantment they offer; stories that hold lessons and speak to the deepest parts of our being but are told because they are wonder-full and not because they are going to connect us with any particular angelic awareness or explicit morality. A good story tells a different tale to each listener. So it is with the word work in this chapter: try to hold a sense of wonder and delight in what you do and do not expect anyone else who hears your words to interpret them in quite the same way as yourself.

34

As words can give shape to the world we experience, by describing a thing, so we can pass it on - to friends, neighbours and new generations. Oral traditions need nothing other than words and people to stretch a thread back over the centuries and carry ancient histories to modern people and the stories we tell can equally carry our thoughts and experiences on to people still to come.

The same may be said of many things from music to paintings, sculpture and whole libraries of books, but a spoken story, a song, a poem is a personal moment shared between the teller and the listener, needing nothing but the moment of contact and is all the more magical for its intimacy.

Every word spoken in a magical space has a weight and each word is a thought given shape - not all serious by any means, but, magically, we should be aware that every word spoken introduces a change to the world. This starts to spill over, of course, into everyday life - "say what you mean, if not, don't say anything" can feel like a dismissal of casual conversation but magically, it needs to be true.

We may leave our enchanted place in the spare bedroom but the Otherworld is not restricted to the wardrobe and if you are one thing inside your circle and another outside of it, the spirits notice. With words as our tools, every time we say "I don't believe in fairies" we shake the bond between ourselves and the Otherworld. Sacred animals are always with us - or may drop in at any time, and saluting them on one day and denying them the next is not a stance conducive to long term positive relationships - believe and belong or leave well alone is the bottom line.

This is all getting a bit serious for what is intended to be a cheerful chapter about playing with language. The conclusion is "be careful". Words are a wonder and a delight and a poem you are pleased with is a joyous achievement, but remember those stories of hapless goblins trapped in the patterns of words, making ropes of sand, and the unravelling power of a name, - for instance 'Rumpelstiltskin'. Look at what you say as you say it, or compose it: are you naming your friend, owning them, trapping them, or are your words part of the celebration of your relationship?

To get back to the animals, this chapter rolls out a series of activities about using words initially to shape and record your impressions. It moves on to more complex ideas about chants that help you move from one world to another and that express the growing bond between you and your animal spirits in greater depth.

We shall use words to:

> describe the experience
> explore the experience
> become the animal
> shape a ritual

Describing the experience

1. Words 1

Initially pick a few words out of your head that capture the moment. As you watch an animal or meditate on an image in your mind, find words that touch upon:

> the animal - colour, shape, size, movement: one, some or all of these - the most striking feature?

the incident - watching each other, you watching it, it feeding...

your feelings - what does this wake in you - excitement, fear, peacefulness?

Now take those words and work them into a pattern - it can be helpful to write them as a list then tear that into individual words or phrases and move these around to find rhythms when you speak them. You may want to add a few simple "ands", "the's", "is" and so on, but keep additions to a minimum.

When you find a sequence you are happy with try speaking it aloud and as you say the words recall the image of the animal in your thoughts. You have written your first invocation - a calling that invites the animal spirit into your presence. This spell may grow more in depth and complexity as time goes by, but here is a start to it - a pattern of words that come from your experience of an animal that describe the animal and your reaction to it and combining with the image you hold inside become an invitation to the spirit world.

2. Words 2, in a group

Working with a shared animal image, a group may repeat the above exercise but with each person contributing two or three words about their perception of the scene. As a group they can then turn this into a collective poem, combine it with some appropriate movements perhaps and present this as a small calling ceremony to offer out to the world around them.

3. Words 3, abstract it a bit more

Words 1 and **2** above are often quite literal statements about animal and experience. You could now play with those words and refine the images a bit more - both sharpening the pattern so that fewer words call up the image for you but also diffusing the whole effect so that others listening and you yourself, may gather a wider set of perceptions from a few words.

In some ways this comes close to writing Haiku, those concise Japanese poems that you may like to explore as well.

Look at your words, or go back to the original experience, and think of it in terms of:

    a) describing the incident

    b) pausing between description and response - insert a breath in the spoken poem

    c) your response to the moment

So:

> *Black rooks tumbling like rags,*
> *Blown by wind*
> *Cloudy sky*
> *Their excitement moves me*
> *Thrilling*

from Words might become:

> *A handful*
> *Of black rags, thrown*
> *Across the sky*

And also

Rooks in handfuls
Black rags thrown,
Tumbling delight across the sky

4. Wordspirals

A longer sequence that may move your impressions onward more can be brought in. Reach out to your animal spirit - "key" yourself into a starting point with it, perhaps using the poem from **words**.

Visualise the animal. Think shape, texture, the smell of it, its senses.

Stand, and with your hands trace the animal in front of you.

Stand and slide from "neutral" - upright, arms relaxed at your sides, knees slightly bent, feet flat on the ground - into a shape that feels like your animal - a crouch, claws raised, a lifted poise, hoof tipped, wings spread, finger-feathers flared. Try this a few times. Try variations of it, find an "essence" position, that at this moment, seems to reach out to your animal .

From here, start talking - use your words again and go on from there, either internally, or around a room you may go for a walk with your animal - a short journey, and keep talking - What do you see? How do you feel? What does this all bring?

Start writing- this is not a full-scale "path-working" or medicine journey, more a tapping into associations and will often release a whole string of moments leading one on to another. Usually the pattern will run from physical - either animal or environmental descriptions to the qualities that are reflected inwards from the animals presence into ourselves.

List them.

Then write them out again but now in a spiral, winding inwards towards a centre, or from a close centre in a swirling outward curve. If you are working with friends, take it in turn to read your wordspirals to each other and reflect upon the images that you share. The effects of spirals are often quite different when read running inwards compared to outwards - no matter which way they were written.

 Take time to decorate your spiral - add colour and pattern and make yourself an exciting visual embodiment of the experience.

5. Identification chants

Going further, you might like to explore Celtic style "Identification" chants. Here, a sequence of statements can draw you into a number of different experiences. To start with, use a sequence to give you a stronger description of the animal you are working with - pulling together physical description with knowledge of habitat and perhaps your own **correspondences**.

"*I am*" is the key phrase: speak this in your stillness and visualise each phrase as you say it and become, if only for a passing moment, that image. Work on your words so that the sequence moves you deeper into the experience of the animal. For example:

> *I am a snake on a stone,*
>
> *I am a snake in the sun,*
>
> *I am a ripple of gold and black,*
>
> *I am water running with bright eyes,*
>
> *I am the hiss of silence,*
>
> *I am a shadow in the grass.*

You could turn things around a little and identify different bits of your body, bonding those to the animal in stages:

> *My belly touches stone,*
>
> *My back absorbs heat,*
>
> *My colour changes, black on gold,*
>
> *I flow like water,*
>
> *My teeth smile in silence*
>
> *My dark eyes open.*
>
> *I am silence moving, a shadow in the grass.*

This begins to sound like a riddle and indeed old riddles can be good places to play with images. Look at the animal and think sideways - what else is that shape, how does this thing really move, when light hits it what colours do I see? Again if in groups, you could start playing your own riddle games, adding movement to your words to shape your animals. Enjoy.

More repetition can build patterns about the habitat of your chosen animal, or highlight a particular part of its life cycle or a season of the year. Don't worry about rhyme - unless it is done well, trying to make poems rhyme can easily turn what might have been powerful blank verse into tedious doggerel. Repetition of key phrases and keeping to set numbers of syllables lends weight to spoken words used in ceremony. Try it and see:

> *Cold the wind, at the break of winter,*
> *Cold the wind, the branches rustle.*
> *Cold the wind that stirs the leaves,*
> *Cold the wind but the hedgehog dreams.*

To this you could also add music: keep rhythms simple and supportive - a drum or hissing rattle can add pace, heighten the silence between words, add weight to the impact. But do not get carried away - keep the music under control so that the images are still understandable - unless your music is strong enough to deliver image without words - in which case it belongs somewhere else and not in this bit of the book!

Let images grow and take shape - do not try to pack it all into a single line of a verse. Give yourself key phrases, single images that are landmarks in a wide process of identifying with your animal. A single phrase should, with practice, release a whole set of other images. You may well find that your poems become more and more minimal until you may end up with a drum-beat broken by occasional phrases.

6. Song cycles

As your collection of poems, spells or chants grows around a particular animal, you could start to organise them into sets of songs that tell the stories of contact with the animal. Song cycles probably belong more to the third cycle within this book rather than this first one. They will take shape most effectively when you have danced, or masked or otherwise worked more deeply with spirit contacts and where relationships are clearer. They remain here as an example of other things you could do with words as your poems and chants combine with other work to create ritual.

Think of a set of poems as falling into a number of categories.

Part 1: who am I? What am I? Identify the animal - a traditional verse ("*I sall goe until a hare, wi' sorrow and sich mickle care, I sall goe in the devil's name, and while I cam home again*") or one of your earlier pieces may fit in here. Do you want to be explicit here, or would you rather present the animal as a riddle? Introduce mystery.

> "*I am companion to the gods*
> *I can conceive while I am pregnant,*
> *I call the dawn and spring in*
> *I am the advent*" [1]

Part 2: the life of the animal - these poems should take us deeper us into the life of the animal by fixing on specific points or places in that cycle and give us a sense of life as that animal.

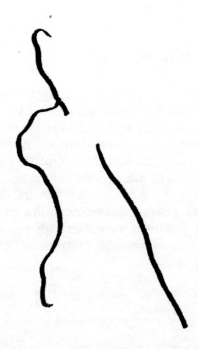

This could also include setting the physical environment - places and times as with the "*Cold the wind...*" verse above. Do not be afraid of grim images here, or of meeting grief - it is all a part of life, and death is a very real force in animal lives.

This section could also bring up threats or dangers beyond the natural everyday ones that the animal faces. If this cycle is part of some protection ritual here you might name the danger that you gather energy to defend against.

> "*Here's the tractor here's the plough,*
> *And where shall we go now*
> *We'll lie in forms as still as the dead*
> *In the open fields the hare said*" [2]

Part 3: power from within and through the animal. Here is power! Here is a celebration of the power that comes with your experience of the animal itself. Strength that is rooted within the species and, through your contact, wakes its own reflection in you - knowing the animal as you will may allow you to tap into the energy that runs through that spirit and also unleash the personal power within you. This section may tap into your own myth system as well, bringing in the correspondences that you accept, or the ones that you have forged with this animal. Most often, it holds a feeling of determination, a recognition that life never gives up, that it survives and persists despite everything. Even if you work with something that usually ends up as someone else's dinner, there is a strong vein of endurance and defiance. Life is lived to the end!

> *"I will run and run forever*
>   *where the wild fields are mine*
> *I'm a symbol of endurance*
>   *running through the mists of time"* [3]

6

Finding Out More

As you start to build relationships with spirits, do not depend solely upon those Otherworld encounters for information on your animal. Root your knowledge of that animal in the physical world as well and find out all you can about it. Tap into the information resources of our society and find books and magazines to read, videos to watch and, whenever possible, animals to observe.

There are increasing numbers of books about specific animals or related groups of animals and while some of these may be overly technical, others are friendly, accessible introductions to the life history of different species. Some such books are listed in the Bibliography - ask for these, and others, in your local library or bookshop.

We shall look at active support for animals in later chapter. While there may be things that you feel the need to do at this early stage with bird boxes, bumblebee and ladybird stacks and occasional piles of leaf-litter, you also need to get to grips with the natural history of your new friends.

You are not setting out to become an expert but you do, at least, need to know that not all big, black birds are ravens and to understand the general areas that your animals move and live in. You need to be able to listen to and wonder about other people and, perhaps, question assumptions and statements based on "nice ideas" rather than on an understanding of the animals themselves.

I met a guided Celtic visualisation once where eels in a river are described as eating salmon, which at once set all sorts of questions in motion that quite upset the working for me as eels do not usually eat salmon...

> - unless, of course, we are in an estuary or still out at sea and are talking about bigger conger or moray eels which are very different animals from our familiar river eels
>
> - or maybe we are looking at young salmon parr on their first run to the sea
>
> - or perhaps eels are going for old and ailing salmon after spawning (although in Britain we do not usually meet the mass die off that happens in some other salmon populations)
>
> - or maybe they meant parasitic, eel-like hagfish but that would still have been at sea
>
> - and all these are exceptions and surely this should have been made clear?

This may sound like splitting hairs, but descriptions of animal behaviour are a reflection of our respect for the animal. Spirits in the Otherworld may do strange things (like communicate with humans!) but essentially they stay true to their animal natures and looking at and learning from animals in the physical world, or in the Otherworld, is based on their behaviour as animals, not on a guise as furry humans (foxes in trousers, rabbits in hats) or on our inventing behaviours to suit ourselves. To start expecting,

Food remains fetish with hazelnuts and fir cones eaten by woodpecker, squirrel, mouse and vole.

or demanding, activity that is foreign to a basic natural history shows a lack of respect for the animals we profess to care about and perhaps a reflection of a human centred view where humans are in charge, humans know what's what, humans have the right to change how other species live.

You will probably find opportunities to meet your animals in the flesh - out of doors, at a zoo, or on a holiday. You may find ways of surrounding yourself with animals: but all those exciting exotic beasties in pet shops need thinking about. Very few wild British animals will turn up in pet shops, although there is an active private trade in captive bred owls. But if you have connected in with a small reptile, parrot, monkey, chinchilla, large spider or squirrel, you may well come across a cousin up for sale.

The conservation issues that come up later in **Fetishes And Power Objects** are also relevant here and regardless of the legal situation, we should still question the trade. "Official" trade in Mediterranean tortoises wrecked populations there before things changed, wild-caught parrots are still decimating tropical populations: your answer has to lie with you and your spirits. For a single animal, you may be able, if you have the experience, money, time and space, to offer it a better life than a short one twitching on the floor of someone else's cage.

If you are an experienced animal carer you may even make a contribution to the support of wild populations with the understanding you may gather about life cycles and breeding patterns. Who knows? This is not the place for a long animal rights discussion about zoos, safari parks and private animal keepers.

To return to the pet-shop, will your purchase of the animal simply create a space into which another will be drawn so that while you may help the life of the individual, for the species as a whole you are helping to perpetuate a difficult, if not unacceptable, situation? Where does all that leave you if the animals have been bred in local captivity: your actions may not have conservation repercussions but can you contribute to the quality of life for the individual? They are not easy questions to answer:

direct contact with your animals is thrilling, but if they are your pets...? I have never managed to settle a lot of these for myself: I will resist and object to importing wild animals for the pet trade, but as soon as I see toads in a pet shop vivarium, all my resolutions crumble and I end up having a ferocious row with myself in the middle of the shop...

So get to know your animals: draw on whatever resources cross your path but remember that nothing matches direct, personal observation if you can in any way do this. Sitting down and watching animals is at least as good a teaching experience as most of the other activities in this book.

7

Travelling

To end this spiral of introductions, encounters and poems, relax from the work and go on an adventure with your new friend.

Set a time limit on your work - maybe use a piece of music of a set length, or use a timer to switch on a radio at the end of your meditation period, or arrange for some kind soul to quietly bring you in a cup of tea and a slice of cake. If you have worked with a sacred space, start in that place, stepping out of it and into a completely different environment if need be. If you do not use sacred spaces, visualise an appropriate habitat for your encounter: start on dry land, even with air and water borne creatures, and walk on into other environments when you are ready.

In your stillness, reach out to your animal and rest the hand of your awareness on her back (the sex of an animal companion is not always clear, nor always relevant, and of course your animal may not have a "back" as such, so just fit in appropriate bits of anatomy). See the animal beside you, regardless of usual differences in size. See, feel, touch your friend.

Look beyond them to their world. Hear the wind in the trees, its touch on your skin, feel the sand beneath your feet, the scent of long grass on the breeze. Go for a walk together.

Keep that contact with your friend and let her take you for a walk through her world. Even if the general area is familiar, you will probably encounter it in unfamiliar ways. Small mammals, birds and beetles all experience your Sunday afternoon woods in very different ways.

Your animal may use different senses from you as it travels through its world. You are still human, however, and working with a human brain that will translate whatever information it receives into terms that you can absorb and understand. So do not be surprised if your butterfly journey still seems to have you looking through your own eyes and hearing things with your own ears. Somewhere along the line, however, the chances are that you will get sudden flashes of a world constructed, perhaps, in layers and trails of scent, with "ghost" images trailing smells across an area and across time. With Toad, now and then, I meet a world built in patterns of temperature, occasional blocks of colour, light and shade and the sudden piercing, hungry clarity of the moving edge of a shape: vision focusses on the front of a limb, or the outline of a turning head that may spell danger or dinner.

Stay with your friend. Travel in her world.

You may stay as a human shaped spirit through this or you may find yourself changing shape to match hers so that, as two fish, you swim together through the sea. Or you may be invited to lie along her back, ride upon her or even be drawn inside her, a passenger of her thoughts rather than her body. With these more intimate contacts, do not presume that you are now in charge. You are a guest. Just because you are sitting on a horse's back does not make you rider and her steed. If she consents to carry you, she will. And she will carry you where she chooses to go.

Travel and learn from the travelling. Do not expect great momentous events to explode around you. The first few occasions like this usually concentrate on movement and exploration of the animal's environment - as if she wants to show you her world. Later, you may find yourself swallowing mice or munching earthworms.

Setting an ending, is one of those times when you must be firm. "It is time to return", or "I must go back now", should be enough to turn you back to your starting point, if you do not find yourself there by the end of your time anyway.

Return. Rest. Record your impressions.

Group work

Within a group, everyone could go on their own personal journey while one member marks time, and perhaps talks, people into and out of their stillness. Or use a drum and set a steady drumbeat that will set the length of the journey and draw everyone back again at the end.

Second Cycle

Connection

Take your first friendships further, get to know the spirits you will work with. Now is a chance to shape links that are both magical and physical and also to explore the polite boundaries of your relationship. When you walk in this cycle, you are being examined, tested and the nature of your intentions and the extent of your respect explored.

Walk in grace, walk with honour.

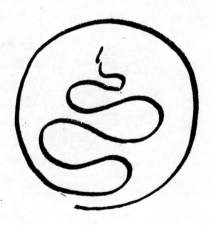

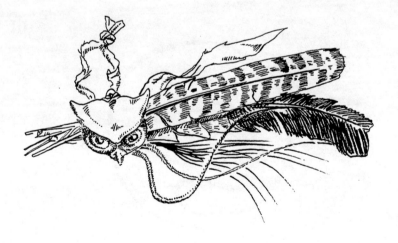

8

Fetishes and Power Objects

"...the touch of bone excites me. The smooth surface of a skull, the hollow curve of an eye-socket, the fringes hanging from ridge and jaw all reach across lives and spaces to touch the life that inspired the skull in my hands, the skull I dance with..."[4]

As you explore connections with animal spirits, you may well want to express the growing bond in physical ways. When you travel, perhaps, you may see a decorated feather on a drum or in your hair, a painted bone. A "power object" serves as a link between self and animal spirit: something found and worked over or a thing shaped from scratch. Usually it is fairly simple and often quite small - something to wear or carry with ease.

Traditionally, power objects usually provide a direct contact with the animal in question, containing some part of the animal itself - dried bones or skin making up the whole of the object or perhaps hair, feathers or shells attached to something else. This is still the usual pattern that we see, but if you come across something else that gives you the contact you need, do not shy away from it because it is "artificial". Numbers of such fetishes may be gathered together into bundles - their collective power growing as items are combined. Larger items like masks

Decorated guillemot skull

and costumes can act as bundles in their own right and will be encountered in later chapters.

You do not need to rush off and make lots of things all at once, when you are ready, the dreams will come. Even if you are not consciously aware of "being ready", at some point, the animal connection starts dropping things into your lap. Plastic frogs from everyone who knows me is one of my regulars. Take it as a signal and "go physical".

Finding Things

A long time as a naturalist has left me with a frightening readiness to pick over old road casualties and wind-scoured sheep skeletons on lonely hillsides. Once you open your eyes, there are things to be found everywhere: feathers, shells, hair, twigs, leaves, bits of string, footprints may all appeal.

In taking from the dead, I choose what calls out to me: touch, feel, sense, select and then offer a prayer of release and thanks to the spirit who has left these remains behind. If feasible, I usually move bodies off roads to a place where they can decay in relative peace: I do not however, bury animal bodies - it feels unnatural and unnecessary (sexton beetles will do any burying that is needed), except maybe in small gardens or to keep something undisturbed to be returned to later and a skull retrieved.

Or you may hunt through more modern avenues: I have a valued set of plastic animals and have shared ceremonies of joy and wild delight with a cuddly toy gorilla. These can still be links between yourself and your spirit friends - do not dismiss something just because it is not "traditional" or ethnic enough. I try to stay open-minded and to consider whatever I encounter. I do not use it all - some of those plastic frogs are altogether too tasteless - but I love my rubber snakes and cardboard fish.

You may have a dream to work from and go looking for a particular item, or you may find it more exciting just to wander with your senses buzzing and find the shape of your animal in a dry twig or its face in a stone. Or just wait and see what comes your way (more plastic frogs!).

Buying Things

Rather than hunting out something potentially smelly from a local hedgerow, you may come across a bone or feather or some other natural thing in a shop that woos you with its elegance. Before buying it, there are several important questions that I would want to answer for myself. When I find something on a walk I may be reasonably sure of the where and how of its death but something bought over a shop counter or in a market place might have a much more dubious pedigree:

has this animal died solely to serve my ends?

is this from a renewable source? - moulted feathers, nail trimmings, tail cuttings - or a side product, making sure that all of an animal who has died is being used.

if it was a captive or domesticated animal, did it live and die in ways that respected its life in the first place?

is it clear what animal this thing actually came from? - among the more obvious confusions are dyed turkey feathers being sold off as "eagle" (of course, in some systems, turkeys are described as "eagles of the woods" but this is stretching the point).

if I am sure of the species involved, what is its conservation status? It is bad enough to hold the skull of an animal that has died just to meet my demands for an exciting ritual object, let alone to then realise that the one that died is one of the last of its people.

Conservation Issues

Most British vertebrates (birds, mammals, amphibians and reptiles, but we are not always too hot on our fish) and some invertebrates (everything else) are protected to some degree under one or another of various wildlife acts. Assuming that you are not likely to set out to kill the animals you want to work with but are more likely to find remains and work with those, it is illegal to obtain any wild bird eggs, to purchase skins or feathers of protected birds, mammals or reptiles or to disturb bats, badgers, some birds, natterjack toads, great crested newts, smooth snakes and sand lizards.

While you could be prosecuted for possessing some remains that you may have found quite innocently by a road-side if you have kept a record of what you found and where and when you would probably be all right, (do not quote me on that). Finding and then trying to sell remains from endangered animals is, however, much more likely to attract attention. No matter how innocently you may be doing this, moving precious items, like eagle feathers, around creates a market into which less scrupulous people could easily step. There is, of course, an argument that says possession and display of any animal product may create a market for the exploitation of that species.

This is a proven effect - take a look at fashions in exotic pets and unfortunate animals rushed home out of petshops and abandoned later. Forlorn colonies of American terrapins in so many ponds in our city parks are legacies of earlier trends.

Answering this is difficult, because the stand that we speak from is one rooted in faith and the object you hold is an expression of your commitment to and relationship with the animal in question. It should be a statement of

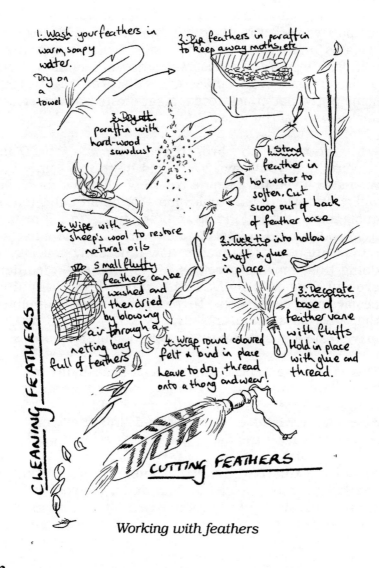

1. Wash your feathers in warm soapy water.
Dry on a towel

2. Dip feathers in paraffin to keep away moths, etc

3. Dust off paraffin with hard-wood sawdust

4. Wipe with sheep's wool to restore natural oils

Small fluffy feathers can be washed and then dried by blowing air through a netting bag full of feathers

1. Stand feather in hot water to soften. Cut scoop out of back of feather base

2. Tuck tip into hollow shaft & glue in place

3. Decorate base of feather vane with fluffs Hold in place with glue and thread.

4. Wrap round coloured felt & bind in place Leave to dry, thread onto a thong and wear!

CLEANING FEATHERS

CUTTING FEATHERS

Working with feathers

support, not of exploitation. It may be that your power objects will need to become parts of the medicine bundles, wrapped away from sight and only revealed on rare ceremonial occasions and often only to small groups of trustworthy people. We are far from the situation in the States where some Native Americans have their rights to possess eagle feathers as religious objects recognised by the state, although collection of these is then only permitted under license.

Another twist on this whole situation may arise if you see yourself as a committed anarchist and do not really care a mouse's whisker what the government or any passing official thinks of what you wear and how you carry it, and if you have the skin of a raven to wear on your head you will do so regardless, thank you very much. While I sympathise with that stance deeply, I would answer that our wildlife laws, inadequate and ineffective though they may seem at times, are the only ones we have and if we are out to protect the animals whose spirits we work with, it is up to us to work with those laws, and with greater and more potent commitment than they can offer as well, not to abandon them just because we think we are better judges of what should be done. They are a tool to be used for protection, do not discard them.

There is an agreement called *The Convention on International Trade in Endangered Species*, or CITES for short, that attempts to control the movement of both live animals and products derived from them, like carved ivory, between countries. While the lists of species covered are lengthy and animals can be moved from one Appendix and hence one degree of protection, to another at times, if you are particularly involved with an animal that you feel may be on those lists, go investigating.

A local library may have copies of *Checklists of Endangered Species* or similar records: get to know if "your" animals are covered and watch out for their presence after that in shops and on stalls. Cause trouble. If a trader has legitimately obtained the articles on sale, there should be documentation - if not, complain. Traders themselves may not realise what they are selling and may respond to gentle comments, or be grievously embarrassed by louder comments about endangered animals being sold in pieces on their stall, or you may feel the need to stronger action. To this end, try contacting one of the organisations in the appendix. Of course, the presence of any dead animal, endangered or not, on a shop stall should be a cause for some concern and investigation...

It might be worth considering the sources of some of the commoner products that we meet. What has died to arrive on this shop-counter? Or if you have found something, how should you clean and protect it:

feathers: shop-sold ones are probably from dead birds, wild ones are usually obviously moulted or from dead flesh. For treatment, see the box below.

bones and skulls: dead animals only - occasional lizard tails may be discarded ones but those are rarely found! Found bones should be washed clean in warm soapy water - if a lot of flesh still adheres to them, try leaving them somewhere exposed but protected from dogs or rats to rot clean, or in the spring suspend them in a pond with lots of tadpoles. On the whole, it is better to leave them until most of the flesh has gone before bringing them home at all. When clean you might drop them in a bucket of weak bleach to whiten them, but do not leave them in too long or it weakens the bone. Check for loose teeth and glue these in place.

shells: like bones, the presence of a mollusc shell means that the animal has died. There is a large trade in the shells of exotic snails and bivalves that is causing major problems with wild populations: in general do not buy them. They are beautiful but the living animals are more so. Found ones can be washed in warm soapy water and left to dry - or soaked and fleshy remains picked off with a strong needle.

crab shells: and some other marine materials, may come from a skin-change as these animals moult regularly as they grow but this is unlikely as a source of found or sold items - otherwise treat as shells above.

antlers: are made of bone, but are grown and shed annually by deer. Coming across them is not always easy but ones that have been shed do turn up (usually on their own, not in pairs). Bought ones may be shed but any bits of skull at the base would indicate otherwise! On the whole, they are shed clean, but may need a bit of a scrub.

horns: are made of keratin (the same stuff as human fingernails) over a living bony core. Lost very rarely through accident, they will usually be found still attached to skulls (they loosen and will slip off as skulls dry out). Farm animals that are to be "de-horned" usually have this done when quite young and horns are small. Sale ones are almost always from dead animals.

hooves: try cutting your own foot off and see how renewable a resource that is. Hoof parings may turn up occasionally, but most sale items are from dead animals. Collections of hooves as rattles are often made as a by-product from the slaughter of sheep or goats for meat.

skins and leather: someone has died. Tanning skins is too complex a process to go into here: fresh skins may be preserved by scraping the inside clean of flesh and rubbing salt or borax onto the inner surface. Peg out on a board to stretch flat and leave somewhere warm, dry and away from flies to dry. You could do the same with fresh bird wings.

teeth: as with hooves and horns for the most part: finding the occasional dropped one would be a real triumph and no trader is really likely to wander around waiting for lions to lose theirs.

hair and fur: tufts and strands turn up in all sorts of places: look along fences - watching, too, for where fox or badger tracks run under a fence line.

Carved frog fetish: bone and brass beads

Hair tufts for sale will depend upon the animal they come from. May need washing and then a rub down with oily sheep's wool will help hair keep its gloss and suppleness.

ivory: no, I have never met anyone who has convincingly claimed that ivory can be "harvested" without killing the original owner - that goes for hippo tooth and walrus tusk as well as elephant ivory. At the moment, there should be no new ivory coming onto the international market but there is increasing pressure that countries with elephant populations greater than their national parks and game reserves can support should be able to cull selectively to control the population. The sale of this ivory would in theory then generate revenue to support the local people and local conservation programmes.

reptile skin: sloughed skin is almost colourless: a ghost of the animal itself. Fragile, it is best kept as a fetish folded into a small embroidered bag. Tougher, coloured skins for sale will have been peeled from the flesh of an animal that one can only hope was dead at the time, although with snakes this is not always the case.

footprints: people do not often sell them, so go and seek them out for yourself. With some water, a bag of plaster of paris, a plastic cup and some cardboard to make a wall around a print, you could make plaster casts of all your favourite footprints and develop a new line in power objects.

Making Things

When you have found some thing, or a collection of things that call out to you, keep your plans simple.

Usually a power object will involve a direct physical link with your animal - that is, you will always have a bit of the animal in your hand - or its likeness shaped out of some other material. Associated with this may be items that reflect its lifestyle, habitat, colouring, nature, or even those indefinable features that you perceive in your relationship that say, perhaps, for you that blue is the colour that links you to the owl.

For the simplest of objects, gather your bits together and tie them into a bundle - choose a thread with care and colour and make a tuft of feathers, a tassel of pony hair and grass, a shell on a thong, a dried toad in a small pouch...The limits here lie more in your imagination than elsewhere - start with ideas that are easy to do and if you find you want to be more adventurous later then reach out for that when you are ready. The difference between cutting and decorating a single feather and making a full "war-bonnet" is one of scale more than anything else and that lone feather may carry as much weight for you as the other.

A lot of traditional power objects contain the remains of whole animals, often bound up in cloth with just a head, or head and claws showing. If you plan to do this make sure your animal is thoroughly dried out and then well bound in cloth. Remember that if it gets damp at all it is likely to start to rot and that hygiene and preservation will always be an issue in damp British weather! One alternative is to work with a skin with the head (and claws or wings) still attached but with most of the body removed. Overall, these can be difficult items to make and store and despite their power and presence might well be things for drier climes than these.

You might choose to work with other materials as well - a stone may suggest your animal's shape, like Blackfoot Iniskim: buffalo stones, or you may buy a stylised Zuni fetish, a Japanese Netsuke, or fashion for yourself something from clay or wood, and then add your hair tassels or hang decorated feathers from it. For myself, I like to find holed flints and then string these with feather, hair or shell.

Getting Bigger

Listen to the unfolding of a medicine bundle where many powers are joined in a collection that is passed from one generation to the next, passing connections and routes to awareness from one age to another...

> "The Home Gun Beaver Bundle was sold to me by Maggie Home Gun Scarcee Man because no-one knew its ceremony and she was apprehensve that it would be stolen from her home and sold piece by piece...Hudson's Bay blanket...skin bag with Iniskims (buffalo stones)...bag with dry powder facial paint...buffalo robe wrapping for contents of bundle, white swan head and neck, badger skin, bird skins, beaver-chewed sticks, canvasback duck, small beaded bag, animal skins, duck skins, two loon skins, beaver skin, eagle-wing fan...berry soup bowl, bag with many sweetgrass braids." (bundle contents list selected from a total of 21 items)[5]

A bundle is a collection of power objects. A package gathered and guarded over the years and accumulating its own aura and presence. Bundles, whether individual or belonging to a family, a clan or even a particular ritual are sacred things. Never opened casually and often attended by special songs and ceremonial, they bring the mixed energy of their contents to an occasion and if the songs that unlock the presence of the bundle are lost, the whole thing may collapse, magically, and become simply a heap of odd bits of things.

As you develop your animal spirit links, you may well find that a bundle grows naturally. We all seem to end up with collections of power objects - some of these remain as fairly "public" ones - things added to a dancing robe, perhaps, or a favoured drum or staff but others expect to remain concealed. The decision usually takes shape as you make and work with an object: it is part of the dynamic that links spirit and self through the object and the energy that becomes invested in the thing itself. So you may find that some objects need to be wrapped and tucked away out of sight until specific times when they are needed - or when your spirit friends call for them to be taken out and danced, or sung.

Shields are another possible development of your smaller medicine objects. Like a bundle, a shield may become the focus of a collection of other items that are bound onto it or hang from it. Although not always painted, the shield surface is usually decorated with an image that draws animal and human together: a picture of the animal, its footprints, a pattern caught out of a vision that displays the power that animal carries with it.

As with many other things here, the limits are those you set yourself and there is not space here to go in detail into the intricacies of shield making. You could start for yourself with something as simple as a hardboard or plywood disc, square, kite or iron shape and work from this. Hardboard shapes can be shaped gently over curved inner sections where hand straps could be added. Native American style shields are usually made of rawhide, stretched over a round frame: try this with wet leather pulled tight over a braced hoop of willow or hazel, or skin shrunk and hardened by heat to make a curved surface (look out "*The Complete How-to Book of Indiancraft*" and "*Mystic Warriors of the Plains*" from the **Bibliography** for practical details).

Medicine shields may be simpler with a painted disc supported inside a decorated hoop (see "Story shields" in "*Talking to the Earth*"). Shields may be kept covered until use and the shield-cover might also be decorated with signs and objects that reflect and complement the power contained within the shield itself. You might also try working with long, curved rectangular bark shields or glue-soaked canvas pulled over pointed oval frames. The options go on unfolding. The important thing for you to do would be to find a shield in your travelling somewhere and carry the image of this back with you to inspire the making of the finished object.

Whatever you plan to do, however, before you get too carried away, you should perhaps ask permission of the spirits involved for use of these things you have gathered.

Kakapo

9

Asking Permission

"*Each animal has its own Master Spirit which owns all the animals of its kind...so all the animals are like children of the Master Spirit that owns them. It is just like a large family.*"[6]

In our short-sighted human way, it is very easy to find a thing, shape it into something more and blithely assume that the spirits connected with it are going to be flattered by our attentions. They may well be, but we should not take this for granted.

Remember to ask permission for your use of an object - either when you find a thing or, soon, when you set it aside prior to working it.

be honest.

be clear about what you hope to achieve with this work - it does not need to be a definite function, it may simply be to strengthen a bond, draw yourselves closer together.

ask for permission to use this object, this thing here in your hands.

ask for blessing and the grace to make and work with clarity, inspired by and infused with the energy of the animal awareness that flows through the thing you will make.

offer something in return.

ꝼox, Fox anꝺ FOX

In ceremony here, you may find yourself reaching out to an individual spirit: the animal whose parts you are using, or your particular friend among all the spirits that are "fox". But you may well also find that you are facing that "Master Spirit" described above by Raining Bird.

There is a series of steps that runs from "individual spirit" - a single fox spirit attached, now or once, to a particular body (the animal equivalent of yourself perhaps) - to a group spirit - the collective presence of all the animals of an area: "Fox" who speaks for all the foxes of your home territory - to FOX who is the voice of all foxes of that kind.

On the whole, I find that animals see themselves much more as part of a spirit collective than as individuals - I am more likely to meet Fox than fox, and that as such, the living and dying of an individual is of less importance than the survival of the population as a whole. But that is just my experience, some friends find they meet individual spirits on most occasions where I meet the collective. Sooner or later, however, you will meet FOX and that is not a meeting it is easy to prepare for, or to anticipate.

The guidelines in this chapter about respect, integrity and honesty and a readiness to have your emotions thoroughly trampled are important. You can always stop, step back and switch off, but if you are walking this path with determination, sooner or later you will have to meet FOX, or her equivalent. Or she may come looking for you one day in the Otherworld if you play with her people but will not stay to talk to her.

Be prepared to give of yourself in return for the claim you make on this object: what your offering may be will vary depending upon your self and your circumstances but it must be made with a genuine compassion and respect. A prayer offered on a rising spiral of incense smoke may be enough or a time of quiet communion with the spirit of that animal may be all that is called for, or you may find yourself being drawn towards a stronger statement. With "cast" items - moulted feathers or hair picked from a fence, a prayer offering is usually enough. With things that have come to you through their death, more may be demanded and here usually you must offer some element of your own life as token of your commitment to the bond you make.

Some hardy individuals will open a cut and return blood to the earth (and be hygienic, for goodness sake), others drum, or sing, or write their thoughts and hopes on paper and burn or bury this with due ceremony. I dance: dance until I meet the spirits involved and dance with them, moving through their experiences and through their demands and expectations until we reach a point of understanding and cooperation that allows me to use the things in question and us all to move forward.

How you conduct such a ceremony will depend upon your usual ways of working, but the experiences within the ceremony will probably show several phases:

> **1) opening:** offering to a waiting silence - like playing to a theatre without knowing if any audience is going to show

2) "seeing" the spirit: the Presence of that animal comes - still remote, observing, deliberating - is this person genuine?

3) moving through the object: accepting the weight of the lives that ended to release the object one holds - you may meet sudden images of living, shocking death or frustration at lives thwarted, or the joy of flight, or swimming and the crash of waves on a shore, the invigorating rush of a stream over your gills - the coming of "fox".

4) the arrival: if you perform with conviction and the spirit approves, it may come close and the ceremony may end with singing, or drumming or dancing you and that spirit together and being shown the use the spirits would prefer you to make of the power object, the shape it should be given, the blessing that lies in its bones. "fox" becomes "Fox", becomes "FOX".

5) the aftermath: the process is often an emotional one - it may be rather traumatic at times but after you have closed the ceremony and had time to relax and absorb, the lasting impression after a successful bid for approval holds a lot of warmth and a feeling of trials passed and lives shared, experiences filtering down through your being that leave you richer and more full of conviction and joy than before.

While feathers and the like and even the remains of whole animals that move in and out of life very quickly may be only a ripple in consciousness, those deeper movements are powerful occasions. They are not to be undertaken lightly: you must know and understand your need for the object and honour and respect the spirit that lies beyond it and be ready to accept what that spirit expects: or be prepared to gather your courage and walk away from it.

You should also be ready to be refused: your intentions may not be welcomed, or maybe the spirits just do not want those items touched. Depending upon the material involved and the nature of the rejection, I will usually let a thing lie and ask again after a month or two and if the answer is still no, either return the object to the wild or make a gift of it to someone whose seems more in keeping with the energy I met during my working: I might only have been involved as a carrier to move something on to the appropriate person.

If none of this seems right, thank, apologise to and return the things you have found to the wild and do not walk that path again until you are quite sure you are ready. We rarely need lots of power objects. Look carefully at the people who festoon themselves and their homes with lots of exciting dangly bits and ask, "Why?" Over time, power objects do accumulate and there is nothing wrong in that, but do not set out on this path by buying, or making, a motley "instant shaman's kit" of feather, bone, shell and skull. Let it happen.

10

Totems and Etiquette

Relationships with animal spirits can take many forms: from fleeting encounters to long term connections, occasional contacts to constant companionship. A confusion of terms has grown up to describe these patterns - animal guide, spirit helper, spirit guide, power animal, totem. Getting too caught up in defining what role a spirit is fulfilling can blind you to what the spirit itself feels it is there to do.

It may be easier to think of encounters in the Otherworld as if in everyday life.

> ...there are some people you meet briefly, a passing stranger you make eye-contact with at a bus-stop or exchange the time of day with in a shopping queue

> ...there are acquaintances you see occasionally, meet now and then, share an experience with

> ...there are your friends, drawing closer to your Self: the people who support you and whom you support, who you laugh with and have adventures with

...and then there are the people pressed closest to your heart: your blood family, perhaps, or the surrogate family that grows through love, people who share your life more intimately than almost anyone else

...and, rarely, perhaps, there is that person who stands beside you, who makes you complete, who knows you and is a part of you - the soul companion whose absence from your life, once found, seems inconceivable

If you look at the spirits you meet in similar terms, as encounters, acquaintances, friends, family and "soul-companions", the development of relationships can make more sense. Human friendships tend to start as "encounters" and work their way along the line, and so it is with spirits: casual contacts may pass on and never be met with again or may linger and develop further.

Some friendships, of course, also arrive readymade with a bang somewhere right inside you. Most terminology relates to "friends", "family" and "soul-companions" - "power animals", "guides" and "helpers" are all perhaps "friends" or "family": spirits who meet you, stay with you for a while, work with you, share their experiences with you, and their power and then move on - or stay. They may enter your life in response to your need (whether you have recognised it or not), or their own, or simply because they saw a kindred flame to dance with in the light of your spirit in the Otherworld.

Do not make the mistake of assuming that any spirit you meet is there because you need, or want, them. The world is alive with spirits and while we do not see all of them, we will meet some of them. They are leading their own lives and the area of overlap between that life and your own is a matter for both parties to determine. Like a friendship, this is not really something to sit down and negotiate but needs to evolve as you and the spirits all get to know each other.

Respect spirit judgment in this: they may see you, as spirit, much more clearly than you yourself do and a difficult relationship is not necessarily one to give up on: the spirits that challenge us most are often the ones, in the end, we learn most from. Equally, do not be passive: nothing can take your rights as an individual away unless you invite them to. Do not let yourself be haunted by stray weasels. Discipline stands: "earth" yourself firmly after visits with spirits. Do not be surprised (or blame yourself) when, nevertheless, a continued presence touches the edge of your consciousness in the days that follow. In exploring spirit contacts, we open doorways into our lives and while you may close your door again, there is nothing to stop an inquisitive spirit looking through the keyhole and shouting,"Ere! What you doin'?"

And after all that, you can still find yourself turning round and discovering a moose wandering though your needlework class. You can say, politely and firmly, and probably silently, "This is not appropriate. Please leave". Spirits are strong and their presence in your life is a measure of their interest in you. They are around us all the time, maybe the ones that you are aware of are the ones who are most keen to be involved with you.

But it can still be confusing, distracting and downright annoying. Practise closing your own doors - earth yourself, ask people to leave - if they ignore you completely it is probably you that have not closed your "spirit watching eyes" fully and are sensing beings that would be passing through anyway, rather than being visited by your own particular friends.

If anyone ever said to you that a magical world would be an easy one to live in, they were lying. It is very simple really - "everything is alive" - but keeping the awareness of that under control and yourself functioning in modern western society can be a tightrope compromise.

"Power animals", then, are friends - members of a new extended family. They bring their own strengths, weaknesses and perspectives to share with you and the bond between you may last for years, or only for a short while depending upon what either party needs to learn from the other. They may move on while you are still revelling in the contact and thinking this the start of a wonderful friendship. If you feel this happening, talk to them - they are not always correct, nor do they always appreciate human needs or timescales. You may find that the friendship lasts but within cycles: swallow spirits may only prove accessible while the birds themselves are here in the summer months, or is renewed under particular, occasional circumstances.

When I am ill, I am visited by two puff-adder spirits I first encountered in Malawi in Central Africa. I only meet them at these times and they bring their own distinctive healing presence and however much I have asked to work with them at healthier, livelier, times, they do not return. All the same, sometimes, it is time for friends to part and when that happens, try to do so gracefully: tantrums and howling storms of tears do not impress spirits very much.

Some teachers guide people in calling to their "power animals" - identifying their human need and calling a suitable animal from a defined mythology to fulfil that and then commanding the situation and relationship once it begins.

I tend to approach things from a different stance and if I feel I need support or guidance on an issue, it will be the need itself, not the name of a chosen animal, that I throw to the winds of the Otherworld, and then let follow what will. I find the unpredictability rewarding and learn more from whoever answers the cry than from someone whom I feel should come, and if the call goes all unanswered that challenges the whole position completely. Perhaps my "need" itself is the illusion that should be shattered. It is that old line again that we can learn as much of grace from a pigeon as a swan, strength from a harvest mouse as a bull and gentleness may come on the soft touch of an elephant's trunk - or the sandpaper caress of a puff-adder's scales.

What animals and where?

Given that I tend to avoid drawing boundaries on experiences, to try to "pin down" possible animals seems a bit contradictory, or even downright unpleasant. If we go into a situation ready to work with whoever comes

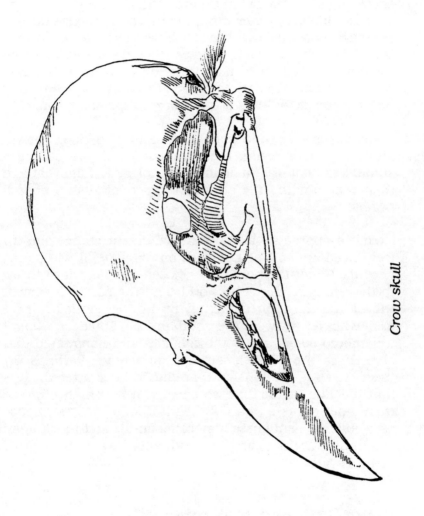

Crow skull

hopping through the undergrowth, it can be very difficult to decide what is "appropriate".

In general, however, I recommend people to work in Otherworld spaces whose equivalent terrain they already know in their everyday lives, or in environments that belong somewhere to the land they are now living on. With that in mind, we tend to encounter the animals living on that land - or those who have been lost relatively recently. So, in Britain we might meet anything from the hedgehogs and stag beetles, slugs, hares and crows of our modern land or the wolves and bears that have been lost only in the last thousand years or so.

We may be unlikely to meet wolves these days outside of a zoo or wildlife park, but their spirits still run in the Otherworld. The hills have barely had time to breathe in the years since the last wolf was hunted or the last beaver trapped. The hills still remember them - they are still in the Dream the land dreams and so we meet them in the Otherworld.

Some animals will still come cruising through, blithely ignoring all bounds of geography or physical space - a whale shark swimming through a small pool, in one instance. If they are not "just passing through", but expect you to work with them, then that is what you do.

But what about totems?

The power animal pattern changes again, sinks deeper, if you find your totem. If you enter this work without a clear impression of what your totem might be, do not clasp the first spirit you meet to your bosom as your long lost totemic symbol. You may find yourself clutching a rather startled porcupine. Have patience. Make friends. Don't fall madly in love with the first stranger who smiles at you. All that sensible human interaction advice that parents offer and is usually ignored also applies here.

Once found, totems are unlikely to change. Other spirit friendships may come and go, but a true totem bond will last. These are the 'family" and "soul-companion" elements of the earlier example. So take your time and trust your feet to find the path to follow. As ever, do not go out there demanding this or that totem. You may meet only a disheartening silence. They may just answer your call and a confrontation with a spirit who feels irritated or worse by being "summoned" is to be avoided. So, work and wait and see who wakes the warmth that fills your heart. And do not be disappointed if you find a sparrow is your totem, or a mouse or a cheerful if rather overweight pig. "Disappointment" does not, in the end, feature: if the spirit you meet is your totem, you have little intellectual hope of

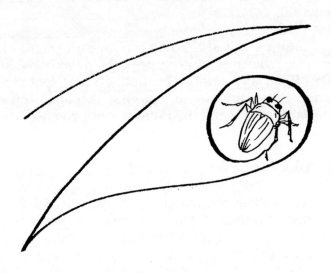

resisting the emotional surge that delights in the connection.

How do you know your totem?

Your totem makes you complete. It is rarely a nice straightforward "Oh, I'm very earth and water so I need a totem all fire and air. I'll have an eagle, thank you". Nor is it always an obvious physical relationship, "I'm big and broad so I ought to have a bear". I find it hard to be precise about the nature of an active totem bond: so perhaps I should describe my own:

> Toad sits inside me - I can drop a hand at any time and touch a lumpy toad head, sitting somewhere in my abdomen. We are part of each other - our spirits dream separately and together. We dance together. Always there, he is not always obvious in my magic - I work with and may represent other animals more clearly than Toad. But he is always there - part of the foundation of my strength, and my delight. He lends a distinct Toad vision of life - most human concerns are irrelevant in a world where action is seen as the moving edges of shapes and either means danger or food and Grandmother Toad memories dwell deep in the earth.
>
> We have been together a long time, now. Before ever I had met ideas of totems and spirit powers, I was working with frogs and toads and they lived all over our back garden, and in the house. Amphibians as books, models, ornaments all came my way, and then one day so did Toad, the spirit, and we have been together ever since.
>
> I cannot now conceive of Toad's absence.

Finding your totem?

As usual, there are no definite answers here: everyone meets their totem in their own way. The activities described in this book are designed to develop relationships with spirit animals - one of these may prove to be your totem. Or you may find your awareness of your totem has been growing over the years: an animal that has always been there in your life - as childhood songs. or drawings, or fascinations, pets, photographs, dreams, may have, all the while, been your totem trying to attract your attention. Or a more casual power-animal relationship may deepen over time as the two of you find you fit more closely together. Or perhaps in the profound silence of a Visionquest or some other initiation, your totem comes as a spirit out of the darkness, stalking, and claims you for its own.

More than one totem?

I don't know, is the short answer. Given the intensity of the totem bond, I feel that the answer is usually "no". You may find, however, that you have both a "family" and a "personal" totem and have slightly different relationships with both of these. You will probably also develop a small spirit family: a group of spirits who you work with in different ways, at different times.

Within your family you may find an intriguing menage a trois developing between yourself, your supposed totem and a supposed power animal, but at what point a power animal becomes a totem is anyone's guess and will probably defy any rule anyone makes up about it anyway. On the whole, I expect to find that people build up a family along the friendship/acquaintance lines described above: a number of spirits who come and go, a couple of close friends - "power animals", and eventually the totem that lies close against the heart.

Family totems

In Britain, on the whole, we have lost our family animals. In shamanic cultures, one often finds that groups - families, or whole tribes - have an ongoing relationship with a particular animal spirit. This is a relationship that may reach back through time - perhaps to an origin shared between tribe and animals that led some individual spirits into humans and others into animals, or may stem from some incident where the one helped the other. Within the tribal totem relationship customs, taboos and rituals will have evolved that maintain and reinforce the bond.

Such a clan totem becomes a strong unifying bond for a group - a shared spirit form to experience the Otherworld through, a link to ancestors, an advisor, an identity. Within the group, individuals may also have their own personal totems while still being tapped into the collective tribal one. This sort of awareness seems to have faded in modern Britain but it may still be rewarding to explore your own family roots for traces of such a link. Who knows, you may find the spirit of your family still there, waiting for the connection to be renewed.

You could try:

> **family stories:** ghost dogs - or cats - or birds - are all known to haunt particular families. The totem who comes to claim the spirits of the dying?

> **coats of arms:** perhaps the rampant ferret or sprawled salmon that lies there once carried a

stronger bond for your people. The story behind the image is important - is the animal's presence there a recent vanity, a recollection of some award or deed, or an original statement of the family's identity?

other stories: older libraries are good sources of specific folklore books relating to individual counties. Try to track down stories from your family's "home territory", if you know it or can find it, and look again for those specific references

what does your family name mean? Does it hold its own clues? Do not be all patriarchal here either: remember to follow the same threads back through your mother's family as well

anecdotal information: "Oh, our family has always had a thing about pigs. Grandma kept one in a shed in the garden. We used to take the scraps down to feed it, but Mum and Dad have only porcelain ones on the mantelpiece". Look for links that persist over several generations. This is the Otherworld we are dealing with - signals come through at times in the most unlikely ways!

If you do find the traces of a family totem, set off on a journey of encounter and discovery as with other animal

spirit sources. If you feel you have got nowhere at all, not to worry! Start afresh and perhaps the totem you may eventually meet, will be the beginning of a new line that will run with your family on through future generations.

Keeping it going

All relationships take time to grow and need work to develop. You cannot simply sit back and expect spirit friends to whisk you off on exciting adventures. Your efforts, magical, physical and emotional are needed, too. Start with honesty. Do not demand or control or conceal. Relax and let the shape of your spirit be the shape of your self and set out with your new spirit companion to form a friendship with a bit of substance to it.

Third Cycle

Transformation

Now you are known. Now you are knowing. And now you are stepping into stronger links with spirit, stepping out of being solely human and into moments where animal and human spirits share space together and masked, or costumed may dance, sing or simply be still in each other's presence.

Find the stillness that lies in the heart of the dance and learn to be with the one who shares the dancing with you.

11

Masks and Costume

One path to of identification with a particular spirit lies in the mask or complete outfit that when worn draws spirit and human together in a deep and profound union. When masked, you become the mask and you need to approach magical mask work with that in mind. A mask acts as a conduit for spirit to reach out to spirit.

With time and use, like all power objects, a mask will accumulate its own energy, and become its own link with the spirit it shapes rather than just being a tool dependant upon its user. It gathers its own presence, becoming eyes through which spirit may watch the world at any time, regardless of you, or anyone else, taking hold and using it.

Working with masks and costume creates dramatic ceremonial settings that can propel you further than you might expect: adding shape, texture, sound and new vision to action that transforms you in your heart as well as in your appearance. It can also, however, be restrictive: when masked or costumed, you are, probably, then bound to work with a particular spirit. Without these, you remain free to change and slide from one spirit to another smoothly as a session develops.

Masks and costume will tend to keep you working within a single form. This can feel a bit of a hindrance at times, but it can also help you move through issues that you may not have ever tackled with that form before. In other situations, you might flow from one spirit contact to another as occasions changed, avoiding issues you might rather not face, but masked you will work through whatever arises with that spirit, offering new and unexpected challenges.

That awareness, the presence, that lies in old masks is something that many people can feel. The sense of being watched can unsettle anyone: few people will enter a room with an exposed "powerful" mask and not react in some way. That watchful presence may be handled in various ways. You may choose to make a resting place for your mask; a space on a table, a hook on a wall, where it can watch and be a part of all that goes on around it. Other masks may need covering, only to be revealed in ceremony. A box or bag will keep them safe and when the time comes to bring the mask out into the open, you will feel it singing.

Inevitably, your handling of a mask will depend very much upon the nature of the mask and the presence it brings. Remember that this is your life the mask is entering: do not allow it to dominate you. If you do not want to feel it staring at you day in, day out, put it in a bag somewhere out of the way until you need it.

Making and using masks can come in almost anywhere along the paths we are walking in this book: their effect will vary according to where you are, but at all times they are powerful and often disturbing tools to use.

For early work, especially in exploring movement, masks can help set people free within their bodies. The anonymity, even among friends, and sense of drama that a mask brings can ease the shift from heavy-footed, stiff-jointed self-consciousness into dynamic self-expression.

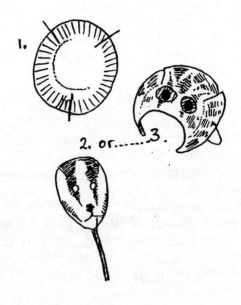

Paper plate masks

parcel tape: gummed brown paper strips. Tear into 5 - 10cm lengths, wet with fingers and build up three or four layers over face and top of head. Leave to dry for 30 - 40 minutes before removing, then leave to dry for a couple of hours before further work (tends to collapse if removed before it has dried enough)

building features: both of these masks need to be kept as light as possible: thin wire, paper towels with PVA glue, and more tape can all be used to build up features and add beaks, snouts, ears and so on. Paint, varnish, add elastic and trimmings.

Wolf mask

Here, working with ready-made masks, either shop-bought, or from some drama-worker's mask box, may be enough. You might still like to make your own mask to play with - it is worth looking at quick techniques to try, recognising that contact at this stage may be with spirits you may not work with again.

As work develops, plans to shape a mask may grow out of work with other power objects - masks can easily become artifacts central to all your power object work, drawing other items into their construction or into a costume that accompanies the mask.

This is not really the place to go into all the possible ways of making a mask to suit your needs. And once more, "Talking to the Earth" has a number of fairly quick mask options. A few other techniques are given below.

When making masks, I usually look for cheap, easy to obtain and work with materials that have minimum environmental impact. This rather cuts out some of the fibreglass and resin-cloth alternatives that are used in theatre. But, as ever, the choice is up to you: it is important to find a medium that you will enjoy exploring, if you are not already familiar with it. Treat your mask-making as a ceremony in its own right: give yourself quiet time to think about it, to do the work and to appreciate what is happening.

1. A real quickie. Take a paper plate and make short (5 - 8cm) incisions at 10, 2 and 6 o'clock round the plate. With the 10 and 2 cuts fold one piece over another and staple into place so that the top of the mask gets a bit of shaping (see illustration). Shape the lower edge of the mask around the 6 o'clock split. Draw a quick, stylised face, add elastic or attach the masks to a stick for you to hold and go out to play. This is a good starting point for mask work - a chance to experiment with a number of different masks before getting involved with a particular one.

2. Working from your face: take a cast direct from your own features and build upon this. Start by giving your face a good greasing (with vaseline, skin cream or oil) and cover hair with a swimming cap, or a plastic bag twisted round and tucked up at the back of your head. You could then use:

> **plaster cloth** - from a model shop, or finer stuff from a chemist. Cut into strips, dipped in water, squeezed out, and then spread in overlapping layers. Keep to a couple of layers, and when half dry, rub surface with fingertips to get a good finish. Leave on for about 20 mintes than remove and leave to dry over-night.

3. Working from a form: use clay, or flour and water paste, to shape the mask you would like to wear on a board, cover the wet form with clingfilm and then papier mache (4 or 5 layers) or plaster cloth (3 layers) the shape you have made.

This gives a chance to build more complicated shapes than working directly from your face. But if you do not work closely with the dimensions of your own head, be ready to make yourself a cloth or cardboard cap to fit inside your new mask so that you can actually wear it. Again paint and varnish before adding trimmings.

If you expect to make several masks of similar sorts, try taking a plaster cloth mould from the form. Varnished and then greased, this could be used again to hold papier mache layers which can be dried and removed to make more masks of the same shape.

Papier mache comes in many shapes and styles. For this sort of work, I usually use PVA glue (available from craft, play or school suppliers) or wall paper paste and water, possibly with newspaper or old Christmas present wrapping paper. The cheaper types of wrappng paper, especially, give a good result when built up in layers. Technically, this is "laminated paper" rather than the pulp of papier mache which you can go off and make a mess with at some other time.

4. Working from a round form: for a whole head mask, you could make a form by building with clay over a chicken wire shape - or over the head of a mannikin or a polystyrene wig stand. Then treat as above, but remember that you may have to cut your mask in half to remove it from the form.

5. Newspaper: light and dramatic whole head shapes can be made from rolled and taped newspaper. This needs a bit of experimenting, but rolls of newspaper can be built up around a cap sitting on someone's head to create large masks. When the desired shape is reached, "skin" the whole thing with tissue paper and a PVA glue and water mix (60:40 glue to water).

For inspiration about designs, colours and everything else, look at books or visit local museums. You might have your own ideas to draw upon anyway but there is such a dazzling wealth of masks forms from cultures all over the world, that having a look at some of their work can add whole dimensions to what you would like to try.

Activating your mask

The activities described in **Dance** could also be used in mask contexts and, yet again, "Talking to the Earth" has fuller notes about developing mask drama - ideas which might be used in a magical context for waking your mask. Masks are essentially "active" objects. They need to be used and with use they will also develop their own identities. Think of your mask as the face of a sleeping being that will wake slowly as it is used. Its waking brings that spirit into the body of the mask so that in putting the mask you meet that personaility and work with it.

Some masks will "go to sleep" when not being worn - others, as described above, stay wake and sleep as they will. You may have set out to fashion a mask with a clear ritual purpose but even so, it is worth "playing" with your mask first, to get to know how it changes you, who comes with the mask and to begin to appreciate the possibilities of that combination of spirit, mask and person. You should find that you will respond to every mask you wear in different ways and different people wearing the same mask in succession will shape different characters. An effective mask transforms you, and invites its presence to come and work with you.

However you set out to use your mask, decide in advance a number of things:

1. The way in: the triggers that prepare you and the mask to work together: stillness, breathing, a movement, a position, a sound. Always be aware with all of your senses of the action of putting on your mask: draw all your attention to the action, do not do it casually. Setting the mask on your head is an act of transformation. Be transformed - and remain yourself.

2. Your purpose: what do you hope to do together, person, mask and spirit? Even if you have met to celebrate the meeting, know that that is what you are up to.

3. Your return: when do you become human again? This may be cued by the end of music, the completion of a ritual, the arrival of someone else, but have a routine that formally ends the mask connection. A reverse of the way in is easiest: "I breathe myself into my mask" and "I breathe myself out of my mask". A simple key like this could also be used by someone else, talking to you if that feels easier.

4. Relax: give yourself time to settle down again: masks call out strong motions in people and alone, or in company, give yourself - and be given - time to relax, talk about it all, have a cup of tea, be touched, or not touched.

Various masks: wolf: fur fabric, spirit: wood, cloth &
feathers, cat: papier mache & cloth, raven: papier mache.

As with mask ideas, notions for changing the rest of your appearance are more likely to grow as other work develops than to spring ready formed on some prescribed "costume-making day". Costume may start to develop as you decide to use ankle bells or bottle-top rattles when you dance, or when, out of some dreaming you bring an image of yourself maned, crested or winged while still human.

The limits to costume are a combination of imagination, resources and practical skills. As ever there are no rights and wrongs at all - the goal is to make a piece that you and spirit feel comfortable with. Such outfits are rarely completed in one go - they tend to go on growing as you use them and they mature as they gradually wear a way along and into the lines of your body.

Outside of the vision that inspires it, a costume may need some thought and careful planning to reach its full effects. In developing your ideas, you might consider:

shape: when you wear this, what shadow will you, should you, do you want to, make? Shoulder fans, crests, manes, anklets, armlets, tails and bracelets all add details and larger features like arm-wings and fan-tailed bustles change overall shape and stance.

movement: do you want to include features that amplify your movements, or complement with their own effects? Again crests and other head-dresses are effective. Tassels, streamers, rags, tails, wings, kilts made of slitted fabric all add to to your movement. The very weight of the materials used will change how you move and will also determine how much skirts or capes will follow your movements.

texture: does your garment change the feel of your skin? There is a sheer delight to be found in the texture of many materials. From the feeling of "putting on something special" to the impact of wearing a different skin over limbs and body, materials used should be considered.

colour: decide if you are looking for realism in colouring your animal costume Or are you, perhaps, drawing upon associations of animal, element and season? Colours tend to become more interpretive as you move from "representational" to "stylised" costume.

Thinking about simple costume, ideas might fall into one of several categories:

1. Body and face painting.

2. Actual/obvious representation: an outfit that is made from, or looks as if made from, pieces of the animal concerned.

3. Stylised: a garment inspired by animal imagery but not necessarily looking like the animal itself.

4. Bits of everything: a composite.

5. "Accessories": rather than a costume style in themselves, "extras" or "trimmings" can be added to finished forms of the above or even stand on ther own as working outfits.

1. Body and face painting

Perhaps the simplest of all transformations but no less potent for that. Sometimes, changing the colours and patterns of our skin is even more profound than wearing a mask - with a mask there is always a physical barrier between ourselves and the world around us, with a painted face it is the transformed you that feels the wind on her skin.

Paints: many brands of face paint are available commercially. Go for palettes or pots of colour rather than cheaper face-paint sticks. Water soluble palettes can give strong colours and good coverage. Invest in a set of brushes (even if you usually use your fingers!) ranging from broad flat-tipped ones to fine ones for adding delicate details. Oil based colours come as traditional grease paint sticks or as palettes and pots (use baby oil, instead of water, and a brush to apply).

Water-based paints are easy to wash off afterwards but oil-based colours are more lasting, less likely to crack and resist the effects of weather. Rain can quickly depress a painted company! For all that, modern water-based colours are quick, striking, easy to use and fine for most occasions.

You could experiment with your own paints. Ash, clay, mud, charcoal or mashed plants may all give colour and could be mixed with a carrier to apply more easily. Water, vegetable oil, lard or egg-white are all possibilities for making a paste to spread your paint - beeswax melted into olive oil gives a thicker ointment base. Some stains are very seasonal; berries and shaggy inkcap ink are autumn delights.

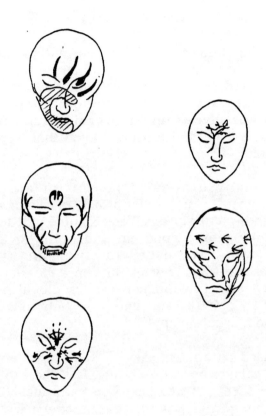

Face painting designs, from top left: bear, deer, coypu and mouse, top right: lizard, bird

Remember that there is more likelihood of using something that will react with the wearer's skin, let alone the rest of their body, here than with commercial paints. Check your plants with care!

Preparation and aftercare: wash the area to be painted with cold water first and pat dry with a towel to close skin pores. With oil-based paints, a layer of make-up foundation can give a good starting base. Do not cover all of a body with paints and even with smaller areas, use natural skin colours as part of your design rather than simply slapping a colour pancake on top of everything else.

Remove paint with warm water and soap, or a skin cleanser, and rub in a skin cream afterwards.

Designs: there are enough face-painting books out now for you to find lots of ideas about painting animal faces over human ones. Key features to work on include the eyes - get the shape of these right and everything else can follow, and the central line of nose and mouth - experiment with lines and shades that thin noses into edged beaks, or flattens and widens them into muzzles.

You do not necessarily need to create an animal face upon a human one to express the human/animal bond. More abstract ideas can be just as effective.

A touch: try a footprint mark, or some other trace of contact. A familiar one is a stylised bear paw design covering a cheek from chin to eye, but you may only need a wolf-print on your brow, or painted antlers or the small shape of a lizard walking along a cheek bone.

A pattern: a set of lines, blocks, curves and dots may also carry the statement you want to make. Draw these perhaps out of meditations; patterns drawn in the sand between you and animal spirit. Look at the body paint of Native Australian and North and South American peoples for ideas to set your own thoughts in motion.

Bits: a body can be decorated with light objects as well - eyelash glue, children's rubber solution glues (the ones that peel off easily with soap!), and vaseline can all be used to incorporate shells, feathers, leaves and the like into designs. Rubber-based glues in particular can be

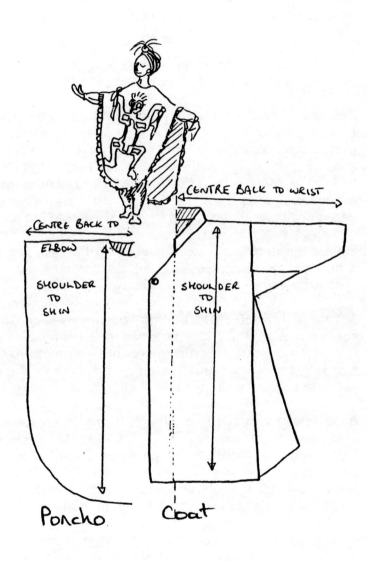

CENTRE BACK TO WRIST

CENTRE BACK TO
ELBOW

SHOULDER
TO
SHIN

SHOULDER
TO
SHIN

Poncho

Coat

Patterns for poncho and Tibetan style coat

worked into short hair and beards, and sometimes it even comes out easily afterwards. (Sometimes it doesn't.) The richer facepaints will also paint over the short hair of beards or cropped heads.

2. Representational costumes

Your costume may develop by drawing directly on the animal concerned. Readily available inspirations here may come from native North American dance and ceremonial wear where buffalo, eagle, bear and other animal costumes can be found. In general, try dreaming or dancing with your animal. Discover what your body feels like then and go on to try to capture that feeling with your costume. As with power objects, once you start looking, useful and surprising additions tend to arrive to add on to your work. If you are not sure what to do, go and rummage through some books and find what excites you. It may well be that to become a bear, all you do need is to wrap your grandmother's old hearthrug round your shoulders, stoop a little and growl a lot. Be aware, however, that this may well end up with passing strangers reckoning that they know exactly what you are involved in, should they see you in costume because your idea has derived from a Native American, or other source. "Oh, she does that Indian stuff," not, necessarily, a problem, but an irritation at times.

As ever, find that balance between planning and making and bear in mind that a costume is rarely finished at one go. If it is going to have a reasonable working life with you, the chances are that it will go on growing over the years so do not rush to finish it all off perfectly - recognise and accept the organic nature of the concepts we are working with.

A useful starting point is to plan along the line of your spine: a simple and effective costume can come with a bristling ridge of fur fabric (spike it up with hair spray if need be) running from nape to buttocks, sewn onto an appropriate colour of long-sleeved top. You could also extend it into a swinging tail - wire this for a bit more strength if wanted. It is often useful to wear dull, dark clothes under a simple costume, this then throws your costume into a brighter light - leggings are useful in revealing your own body but transforming it at the same time.

From this point, you could spread out along shoulders or down over thighs with patches of fabric, punctuating joints with tassels or feathers. Different fabrics can also build up reptile, fish, amphibian or invertebrate outfits - use iridescent leggings!

Another simple step up, is to cut the shape of a hide out of fur fabric (don't get too caught up in the correct lie of fur as it falls from the spine or anything like that) and work that onto your clothes, or sort out crucial strapping points to hold the "skin" against your naked, painted body. Does it need to be sewn down, belted, buckled or left to hang free under a mask to carry the shape and movement presence of the animal you work with?

Wings are often key features that can give lots of trouble. You do not need to make definite "wing" shapes to convey that feeling of flight. You could do so - look at descriptions of North American Eagle Dancer outfits. However, a 3/4 or full circle cloak will also give you a lot of movement and could be decorated with feathers, ribbons, rags or fabric paint. Check the weight of the fabric you want to use to see how it moves - wave it around in the shop first! If your piece of cloth is as wide from centre to edge as you are long from nape to knee, there will be "extra" that may hang over the hands, that could hang as a wide curve between shoulder and wrist loop or have a slender pocket sewn in to take a cane that you will hold, extending the length of your arm and giving you a heron-sweep of wing to work with.

3. Stylised Costume

The outfit you wear, does not need to look like the animal you work with. It can be tricky to create a convincing hedgehog with domestic resources. (But a hedgehog is a delightful shape to work with as a hat!)
You might then look at a design that interprets the animal, rather than represents it. Here, think about what associations go with the animal for you. Go back to those original principles in costume and apply them again. Look at costume from around the world to see where animals have become garments and the way ideas are presented: Tibetan ceremonial wear and blankets from the North-west Coast of North America has much to inspire us here. Two simple designs are illustrated: your final piece, assuming you make it yourself, need only be limited by your sewing skills.

a) simple poncho style: take a rectangle of cloth as wide as your arms spread from wrist to wrist and twice as long as as you are from nape of neck to mid-shin. Cut a hole in the middle of this. Then decide if you want to wear it like this or turn it a little and try it like that. After this, what comes next is entirely up to you: edge it and line the neck hole with cloth of another colour.

Hem this cloth, or slash it to give a fringed border. Draw all over the cloth with fabric paint. Draw all over it with permamnent magic markers if you would rather. Poster paint will run in the rain or the washing machine.

Dancing robe

Applique designs on it (i.e. create a picture by sewing pieces of cloth in layers over the basic garment), or embroider upon it. Long streamers, tassels, and feathers all add movmement. The finished result is easy to make, easy to wear and contains a lot of movement, or can carry a lot of dignity in slower, more statuesque moments.

b) **Tibetan style coat:** use this as a basic garment, working with colour and fabric to carry impressions. Upon this you could gradually build layers adding both dignity when still and movement when danced: tabards, capes, hanging scarves and wings might all develop. Use embroidery, applique or fabric paint to decorate these and try to add features in layers where each layer adds a different texture, shape or movement to the finished piece.

4. Dancing Robes

Combining both stylised and representational ideas, a dancing robe is usually made of leather and is more haphazard in its construction than cloth outfits. It is a basic skin robe upon which you will build bead-work or other patterning (or those permanent marker pens again), add fetishes and power objects and over time build up a garment that feels as if it might get up and walk away on its own. The guidelines about working with leather and dead material given in **Power Objects** and **Asking Permission** apply here as well.

Making clothes with leather is a skill in itself, even with such a structurally simple garment as this. In brief:

work on a large surface

hides in a dancing robe tend to look odd if sewn together like cloth, as you might in a leather shirt or

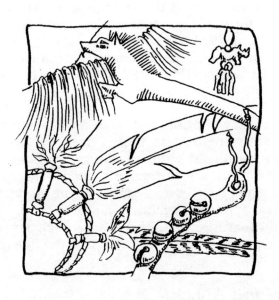

Costume accessories: Anklet: sisal fibre or hair, dance bells; carved horse staff, rhino tassel, feather fan.

trousers, so overlap the edges of skins instead and do not worry too much about the odd, wavering lines of connection

leather will not pin together like cloth so outline where one skin will overlap another with chalk or a thin pen and line them up as you sew - you could also use double-sided tape to hold pieces together

use commercial leather needles - either for hand- or machine- sewing. If hand-sewing, try piercing sewing holes first with a leather awl and use a strong thimble (bleeding over your robe can feel like an appropriate offering but becomes painful after a time) do a double row of stitches if you possibly can, it reinforces the seam line which, with the weight of leather, has to take a lot of strain.

Accessories

Maybe a rather dismissive term for the "extras" that can add so much to an outfit or on their own can give a mask a costumed body to work with. There are lots of things that you could add to either your costume or direct to your body to add sound, movement, shape and colour to your work.

power objects - individual power objects may already lend themselves directly to use here as staffs or sculptures to carry, as necklaces, bracelets or headdresses to wear

anklets and bracelets - fasten bells, bottle-tops, bone, wood or shell to bands for sound or tie rags or wool on bands worn at knee or elbow for weight and movement on lower limbs. "Horsehair" can be improvised from unravelled sisal rope, steamed to straighten it and then looped over a thong and knotted into place with a strong thread.

collars - covering shoulders and upper chest and back might be made from fur, fur-fabric, felt or other cloth. Their edges afford lots of space for hanging things and dressed feathers can be sewn in wing-like fans projecting beyond your shoulders. If you are making a fan like this, you might need to stiffen the underside of your collar with scrim or interfacing from a haberdashery.

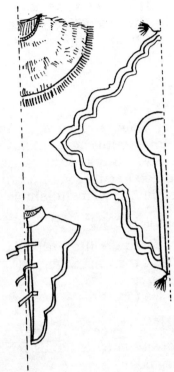

Collar designs: sit separately on top of other clothes

breastplates - embroidered cloth or decorated leather crescents worn on the chest, like a reduced collar in some ways, can make very striking "focal points" for attention and awareness. Hang things from the edge or incorporate items within the decoration - sequins, beads or polished stone "eyes".

fans - the range is endless. Find and paint a traditional folding fan, find a rounded feather fan from a ball gown, make a bird wing fan or a peyote loose feather fan. As well as being power objects in themselves, fans can lengthen the span of your arms and become tools of extra expression, especially with bird dances, adding that feather tremble seen in some courtship that is so hard to capture with fingers.The illustration shows a fan inspired by Inuit dance fans, made of bent willow hoops and dressed feathers.

head-dresses - this list was already extending rapidly and to do any justice to the making of head gear would require a whole extra volume in its own right. Often the ideas will come with the material you have found to work with, combining that perhaps wth inspiration drawn from maybe native American or South-east Asian or Oriental styles. Simple things to try might include: different ways of veiling your head - try a variety of lengths and weights of cloth, with and without bells or other weights at corners and along sides; dressed feathers tied into your hair - singly or hanging in small numbers from a disc of leather; streamers of cloth, fur or decorated leather - fastened just below your crown or from a head-band, decorated bands -a "crown" if you like of cloth with felt or leather shapes added to it, florist wire can be used to make more complex shape of vines, twigs or snakes and felt can be stiffened with varish or paint - or make your crown from climbing plants found in a friend's garden.

Developing

Magical costumes are rarely "finished". They go on accumulating both "bits" and "power" over time. They become power-objects in their own right and like masks, you need to determine how different garments should be treated. Some should be stored away until needed, others might expect to be displayed on a wall between uses.

12

Dance

Dance is a celebration. With dance, we can share a wonderful intimacy with the Spiritworld. Our moving bodies dance across the barriers between the worlds and through the walls of our identity, allowing us to become other beings as we dance. For myself, when I work at the deepest levels of my dance, I share the space my dancing body fills with my spirit family and the shapes my body makes come as combinations of spirits expressing themselves through flesh.

Dance is a gift we can offer the Spiritworld. In a danced ceremony, much of the other work described in this book - song, fetish, mask and costume may all be drawn together. Perhaps because most animals are beings of movement, when we dance them, we often feel them more intensely than at other times. Of course, you may now turn round and go and find exceptions for yourself all over the place, but until you have let yourself dance, do not ever dismiss it! And we can all dance - to dance is not difficult. The difficult bit is letting go of self-consciousness and preconceptions and received notions that "I cannot dance" that may lie alongside the ones saying "I cannot draw" and "I cannot sing".

So. Dance.

As with other exercises, you should start a dance session by relaxing both body and mind. This time you might find it more profitable to explore ways of reaching inner stillness through outer movement, touching upon the stillness that lies at the heart of a moving world.

Set a pattern to your work: relax, warm up, main dance, wind down. If you work with music, choosing your piece with care can help pace the whole activity and these stages in it. Initially, give yourself 20 - 30 minutes of working time and if indoors a few square metres to turn around in.

It is nice to have a lot of room to really throw yourself around, but work with what you can find rather than not at all because nothing hits your ideal. Out of doors, of course, you will have more space but an increased likelihood of visitors. It may take a while to become brazen enough to ignore the curious stares.

I prefer to work with music and the following exercises will be presented as if worked to recorded music - you may chose to work in silence, with ankle or wrist bells or with a willing friend banging a drum. Alter everything to suit your situation.

Choosing Music

The inevitable comment here is "use whatever you like". If you are working alone it is as simple as that, but with a group you will need to find something that most people will respond to. Think of music as a wave that you will lie along to relax and then turn into and dance through, moving with the wave but not controlledby it. It gives pace and sometimes emotional change to any story you may dance but you should not be bound by it.
My guidelines for myself are:

> go for something with layers of sound in it - where a strong rhythm lies that can be followed while other elements of the music would allow people to find other movements within it.

> in group work, avoid lyrics in a language that people know or that may start to tell, or interrupt, the story a person dances.

> dancing alone, be aware that choosing songs you know will produce responses that reflect your

feelings about the song itself - although this will happen with any piece of music as you get to know it - rather than unfolding new experiences.

do not go all proper on your music - use what you enjoy and would jig along to while doing the washing up if it came on the radio, and stuff anyone who says that you can only use something very profound and ethereal to dance magically to.

Relaxing

Use your regular breathing exercises to settle your mind and let everything else start to flow. If possible, try this standing and use your breathing to start your body moving gently.

Warming Up

With regular breathing, arms and body movements come almost automatically. Use your inhalation and exhalation cycle to gradually raise and lower your arms, adding a gentle turn to shoulders and back as you do so. Let this gather its own momentum until an exhalation lets your arms sink to your sides and your whole body to spiral down to a crouch facing behind your original direction. Inhale and uncurl, turning upwards and forwards with your arms rising up and out, opening out your whole body shape.

A thorough warm-up is an essential part of a movement session. It is very important to limber up, and gently loosen joints, muscles and mind rather than jumping straight in and being surprised when you end up with cramps, stitches, pulled muscles and mental confusion.

Aim to work with with each bit of your body, gradually growing more vigorous and covering more ground. Make sure you stretch, turn, curl, travel, crouch, crawl and leap (where possible).

You might:

> start at your head and work your way down the body, rotating, flexing, bending, wiggling and stretching bits as fells appropriate - a ripple of activity that passes down your body.

> start with your whole body all at once, making very small movements - a relaxed but contained dance that gradually spirals outwards, pushing the amount of movement further.

> do a few circle dances drawn from the folk and modern dance repertoire of the Sacred/Circle Dance movement.

> look at the teachings and music of Gabrielle Roth and follow her guidance for a Body Jazz (and explore Roth Five Rhythm or Wave workshops for other developments).

Always be aware of your breath. Feel your breath - with slower movements, try breathing in as you gather yourself for movement and out as you make the movement. You might want to add a sound as you breathe out - a sound that reminds you of the animal you hope to dance with can feel good. Do not worry if this also brings you to laughter. Laughter warms body and spirit alike. I can never whinny convincingly as I always end up giggling. In general only make a sound if you feel inspired to - I usually dance in verbal silence.

Throughout your warm-up, try to let your mind stay relaxed or, if anything, let it settle upon images of the animal you hope to dance with.

Neutral

The concept of a "neutral" position is a useful one to get to know. The idea here is that in a certain position you are still, your body is making no particular statement, standing, poised and ready to act. A position of potential rather than actual energy. Try it: feet shoulder width apart, head up, back straight (but not rigid), knees slightly bent, arms loose by your sides, hands relaxed, breathing regular. A position to move on from, it is also a position to return to.

Practice stepping suddenly out of your dancing and into "neutral" and there let the outer and inner momentum of your dance settle and become accustomed to this as the "place where movement stops". This can, if you like, be an escape route in your dancing: if you want to get away from the tension of it and the passion of it, rather than throwing yourself out of the room in a tantrum, simply stop and step into neutral.

Give yourself time to catch your breath, to calm your thoughts, to reflect and then go and make a cup of tea - or start again.

Another useful starting and stopping point is a curled up egg, stone or foetus shape on the floor. This offers a good form to unfold and evolve out of but is a bit less relaxing than the standing position.

Meeting Animals

Again, as with earlier activities, you do not need to enter a movement session with a clear animal waiting behind your eyes. It may even be better not to do so but to enjoy the movement, to play your body into rhythm and freedom and see what transpires. The activities **Leading your body** and **Having a party** below can both serve to find animals or simply to take warm-ups into more structured movement sequences.

Leading your body

Go for a walk around the space you are in. Walk "normally" to start with but then push different parts of your body to the fore and follow where they lead. Your nose - your chin -elbow - bum - knee - hip - chest - little finger - shoulder blade, they will all take you in different directions in different ways. Discover how your body changes behind it, how your whole movement changes. Do different bits of body produce slower movements, faster, more turns, more lifting or more crouching?

Or you may do it all with your feet: big toe first - heel - ankle - sole - outer edges of both feet - inner edge - ball - backwards - sideways.

Go back to the movement that produced the strongest response in you - the one you enjoyed most, or liked least, and play with it. Repeat it. Exaggerate it. Find several positions that capture the whole experience and repeat them as a sequence - make your own dance.

And do it all without thinking too much about it. Half-close your eyes and bend with it. Relax and invite the animals whose body responds to your movements to come and dance with you. Keep your own movement going, asking yourself "who moves like this?" and feel for the moment when the reach of your arms is touched by the feathers of a wing or a careful step is the positioning of a hoof or the curl of your body is the sway of a tentacle in a wave. There is almost always an animal there. We just need to relax enough for them to step up and be noticed. But, if after all this, you still do not find an animal, enjoy the movement for itself and let yourself dance.

Having a party

Leading your body starts with a movement and goes on from there. This activity starts with a feeling and lets you move around that. Move your way through a cycle of feelings something like this:

start with a party, moving around, smiling, nodding, relaxing into the situation.

happiness - this is your party, you are surrounded by your friends, people it is good to be among, enjoy their company, let your body reflect your happiness.

anger - time goes on however and it grows late and you are getting tired of all these irritating people and you wish they would take a hint and go away and leave you alone! Begin with irritation and grow into anger.

pride - but no, no, you're not going to be angry with them because you know they are not really worth your anger, or even your notice at all, you know you are a much better person than any of them...

fear - pride, however, is often an eggshell mask covering your own insecurity because you know that everyone here is everso much better at everything than you are and you hope that none of them notice you because they are all so much better looking than you are and better at making and doing and being and loving than you could ever be and maybe if you are very careful none of them will even realise you are here at all

shyness - but no, you will not live your life in fear and you gather some small smatterings of courage and reach out with a tentative smile, just a quick exchange, a brief flicker, and it is returned and you feel bolder and push yourself a bit more, and reach out more, and your smile and the smiling of your body becomes wider and more expansive

joy - and your happiness returns, warmer perhaps and more encompassing for the process has changed it

Then, as with **Leading your body**, go back to a particular set of movements, develop them and reach out to an animal.

Touching skin

This takes a different tack, not always as appropriate for a completely open invitation but can be used there or even more easily when you enter the dance with an animal already waiting.

Relax. Hold a hand out at about waist height a little away from your body. Half close your eyes and invite the animal to let your hand rest upon it. Now slowly move your hand. Trace the animal as it stands, lies, hovers, in front of you. Sizes can change but shapes persist, and textures. Move now, following the shapes your hand traces with the rest of your body. Maybe bring up your other hand. Start to move, following the animal, let your body respond to the shapes you find it making.

Definitely one to try with some flowing, sensual music, **Touching skin** may read even more strangely than other activities but offers a warming and powerful little moment.

Take the animal further

Having found an animal to work with, initially just get to know each other through movement:

> **prowl** explore the space you are in through the movements that brought the two of you together.

> **add environments**, seasons, as the music changes.

> **slow** movement right down, slide into slow-motion and feel the shifting balance within your movement - a very valuable experience.

> **break** your movement down into straight lines and corners, sharp movements with abrupt starts and stops, move limbs and body as units. Think "robot". Clicking your tongue to mark starts and stops helps.

> **stop** - be still every so often within your moving, pause and hold the position you are in for a moment then move on.

> **enlarge** your dance to make your movements as expansive as possible.

contained - reverse the above so that your dance is just as varied but occupies as little space as possible.

overall use the changing pace of your music to alter mood and style of movement without changing animal.

These activities all build up ideas to refine the way you are moving. Often the changes are not conscious, but even dancing, we tend to move within our own personal ways and the shapes of our imaginations. Experimenting with other ways of moving can open up new avenues to follow.

Dolphins

The above activities can run either in solo or in group sessions. To close this phase with a group play a relaxed "follow my leader" around your space. Call "Dolphin on...." and the person chosen then leads the group across the space, staying in her animal movement while everyone else copies that one as best they can until she calls the Dolphin onto someone else. When everyone has lead the group, stop, rest and try to identify each other's animals.

Why "Dolphin"? - because the activity is meant to have been inspired by watching dolphins playing this freeform follow my leader through the waves.

After all this, give yourself time to relax, scribble some words, draw colours, shapes, patterns of movement on a scrap of paper. **Touching skin** is a good activity for calling up images for wordspirals.

Winding down

When you reach the end of a session, give yourself time to stop. Relax again. As with other work, thank the animal for its presence. Use whatever means you are comfortable with to earth yourself again. Even if you feel a bit hot and sticky, put on another layer of clothes and make sure you do not get chilled. A shower is nice, too.

In an opening cycle, all the above may be "meeting" activities - opportunities to make initial encounters with spirits and to get to know one another. You may even find that you dance though several animals in quick succession before settling on one to work with. Sometimes it can be hard to find someone among all the movement. You might prefer to "find" an animal with other activities and then use movement as one way of developing that contact.

If you approach movement work like this, the previous activities are still useful as they encourage you to explore what your body can do. More exciting results usually come when you enjoy what you can achieve and the animal comes along and adds a new flavour to that. It can be easy to fall into stereotypes of movements and even crawl around on hands and knees in an automatic "oh, I'm a lion' response. An activity like **party** helps you explore feelings in movements first. You should then go on to interpret the animal rather than be a person pretending to be that animal. It is the difference between "this is what my lion feels like" and "this is what a lion looks like". We are human, our bodies are capable of a huge amount of movement and expression but they remain human and move within their physical compass. I have not yet seen a lion that walks on its knees.

Dance Some More

As you begin to enjoy your dancing, always be aware of where you stop: what are your limits, physically and personally? Try to push these. Gently. Push your movement a bit more, make those stretches a bit longer, get right down there and sprawl, or turn with more vigour. Try to find your own edge of endurance, of daring, of embarrassment and dance upon it.

If you are working with some friends, a partner can help you see your animal and your movement and extend your understanding of what you are doing. The following activities are at their best with a partner but when alone, I dance with shadows and reflections and use these in a similar way.

Reflections

Facing a partner, take it in turns to slowly slip from "neutral" into your dance shapes and back into neutral again. Your partner should reflect back your movements like a figure in a mirror. This is not a competition to outwit your partner, it is a chance for you to watch your animal take shape in someone else and for them to sample the dance you have been working with. Do not tell your partner what to do either: she is a different person, her body will not match yours and you can learn more by watching what happens to her body rather than expecting her to conform to your idea of what you are doing!

Initially, keep this more or less on the spot but when you are both happy, start to move. Along the line of your mirror, this stays as reflections but as soon as you start moving in three dimensions as it were you start to move out of **reflections** and into **conversations**.

Conversations

If we were truly "reflecting" above, partners would get further and further apart as we moved away from our mirror surface - or would be pressed nose to nose and going nowhere. So now move to match or complement each other's movements. Have a conversation.

Firstly, try some sticks: pea sticks (for garden plants) connecting partners, supported by fingertips or palms, right to left, left to right, calm and bring unexpected delight to movement. With slow music they draw wonderful flowing dances full of turns and intricate folds as people turn their couples inside out or in a bigger group try to pour through the arches that others make. And of course those sticks should not fall! (A similar effect can be produced with string with loops to slip over fingers, the aim being to keep the strings taught at all times.)

After a while, separate, pick up extra sticks so that everyone has a pair for themselves and go for a walk, lead by the sticks themselves. Let these become antennae, conductors' batons, the stalked eyes of snails, and follow where the tips of the canes lead. Again, enjoy the grace and flow of movement that tends to grow out of this.

After that, discard the sticks and have another conversation with a partner. Stick activities are good ways of slowing people down and drawing out a sensitivity to how someone else is moving. So now when your partner moves there, be aware that her movement creates a space here that you can flow into. Your movement in its turn should draw your partner into the space you have made so that the two of you start to move like a single fluid whole.

Dancing with auras

If you have done any work with sensing auras, those dynamic energy fields that surround us all, they can be drawn in as stimuli in taking conversation dancing still further.

Think of stroking your partner's animal, and, no, it does not matter if it is a sea anemone that would not normally be stroked!

Start on your own, hands raised, palm to palm, a few centimetres apart. Close your eyes and focus your awareness on your palms. Feel a warmth there, almost a pressure. A fuzzy ball caught between your palms.

Turn now to your partner and gently reach out to meet his hands, palm to palm, a few centimetres apart, and reach for that same feeling of warmth between you. Then start to move, guiding hand by hand. Like **reflections**, initially follow each other's movement, work simultaneously without taking definite turns to lead and be lead but try to anticipate and respond as your partner moves.

Move on from hand connections to slowly run a gentle hand, holding that distance, over a shoulder and arm and let his dancing animal respond to this, just as you respond to his own movement over you. Use this to guide your dance, your travelling hands drawing out reactions in each other without ever making contact. As you grow in confidence this can pick up speed - it may tend to do so anyway depending upon the animals involved - and distance. The "space between" can grow greater as you become more sensitive to the effects that your movement wakes in your dance. With practice, you may find yourself still dancing with your partner while all the length of a room and a company of other dancers separate you.

Respect your partner in this and his feelings - an effective session can wake strong feelings in people. I tend to get all very emotional and need to go away and breathe deeply and quietly for a bit at the end of a good dance. Other people may find the whole experience threatening or intrusive: all those reactions are valid and should be respected. If people want to go on and explore for themselves why they react to such closeness in such ways, that is their choice but should not be expected of or imposed upon them.

Dance out of stillness

Relax into neutral, and as music plays discover how much can be expressed by a sway, a tilt of the head, the lift and fall of hand and arm, a gentle, small-stepped turn. Give yourself a certain upright dignity, feel the line of your spine as central to your movement and draw your dance out of a combination of this and that still place that lies in your heart.

That inner stillness is an important constant, contained movement works as an effective way of finding that while your body is dancing, your heart can become more and more calm amid the movement. Try assuming various "ritual" poses or those inspired by statues. Or anything really. Create gestures that offer honour, that show praise, that express your animal's presence in the tilt of your head, or the way your eyes look sidelong. And all the time keep some element of yourself in motion like some toy that never quite stops moving.

Try it.

Listen for a silence within and slow down and move from that.

Open your stance more and now respond to the world around you, or to the Otherworld that you meet inside of you and with a sliding hand and the changing weight of your body react to this. Trace the lines of tree or rock or let the wind shape your body. Keep it slow, keep it flowing. Explore and return to sets of movements that you can learn and keep as a personal sequence that almost become dance prayers of honour and respect for the world you dance within.

Breath of the Beast

In this set of activities, the "animal" side of our dancing often quietens down and working with a partner becomes more about us as humans exploring our abilities and our sensitivity to and enjoyment in dancing with other people. This is not to be regretted.

Anything that helps us respond with more grace to the people around us, I feel, is a good thing, and when we return to more explicitly animal-inspired dance our responses are finer tuned and the dance benefits from the experience.

If you are new to dance, or even if you have old and experienced feet, going through the earlier activities is still a good way of getting yourself going. And, of course, your dance work does not need to stand alone. It could fit into a working that also involves visualisation, words or music.

But somewhere you need to stop planning, stop exercising and activitying and let it go. Dance in freedom. Dance in joy.

That is easier to say than to do. Here follow another collection of activities, again not intended to be rigorously followed but ideas to give shape and form to your own dance ceremony.

The above activities should all help you develop ways of expressing character and adventure shared between you and your animal through movement. Sometimes, you will want to go further than any of the above seem to allow you, so when you are feeling brave, try **Breath of the Beast** and when you simply want to be set free, **Become Your Animal**.

136

Breath of the Beast

All this dance stuff can come over as very nice, a bit detached, with a whole group of assorted animals cheerfully sharing the same space. And so they do. There is, however, always a wilder side and it is good to let that out now and then. **Breath of the Beast**, inspired by the film *"Nightbreed"* developed as a group exercise to do just that. You can do it on your own but it is not so much fun having a prowl without having someone to prowl after.

Think of your breath. See it as a cloud. As you exhale, snort, hiss, blow out your breath as a cloud that envelopes you, like frosty morning steam. And transforms you. Every breath draws the beast a little more out of its hiding and into your flesh. Hear it snarl.

Start without music, using your breathing to shape the silence. Your breath is the fire that transforms you. Breathe in through your nose and hiss out through your teeth. Close your eyes. See that enchanted cloud billowing around you, swelling and intensifying with each subsequent breath. Your breathing does not need to be especially deep, nor should it be overly fast; it is not the quantity of air you are moving that makes the difference but what you are doing with it! You are not trying to hyperventilate.

In a group, start this together, synchronising breaths for at least the beginning of the event. This sets a collective rhythm that encourages interaction and a certain harmony within movements. This will usually disappear as animals find their own speed and set off. You could, however, set a more formal discipline up from the start so that a still figure, perhaps, with a raised hand will call all to halt and establish the original breathing discipline again. Not as disruptive as it may sound, this allows the

group to align themselves with each and their purpose again and, providing it does not happen more than once or twice in a 20 minute session can propel the whole thing forward again, providing a step up to another energy level.

The breath hisses past your teeth. Feel the change. The eyes in your head open as your own eyes and as your animal's eyes, looking at this world and into the Otherworld. Prowl. Snarl.

138

Do not be afraid - go with the animal in this. **Breath** often brings stronger responses than other activities - the connections feel fiercer, the eyes are brighter. Make sure you do not bite anyone else, or claw or otherwise physically attack a passing lunch: back off, calm down, put your tongue away.

Responses are not always predatory ones - often livelier and Trickster elements are released and the whole occasion can become quite rowdy, especially if a number of smaller animals start winding some of the bigger ones up. Birds are very good at teasing, or ganging up to mob their potential predators.

Breath needs to be carefully controlled: strong music will do this, setting a 10 - 20 minute dance period. A group could have a "watcher", not dancing, who can be relied upon to tap someone on the shoulder and bring them to earth with a bump if they should start gnawing the furniture.

Give yourself a good relaxation time afterwards: a strong **Breath** session leaves everyone feeling both tired but touching a new and vibrant energy.

Becoming the animal

Work through a gradual process of identifying with the animal you hope to dance (usually by this time, you will have a clear idea of who this will be).

> **in silence and stillness**, visualise your animal. See it standing there in the darkness behind your eyes.

> **a chant** or **wordspiral** you have written earlier may help. With each phrase relax your body, sliding step

by step into the shape of the animal you will dance. You might move from neutral, or flow out of a curled egg shape on the floor.

keep your eyes closed and as your body moves see/feel a corresponding overlap with your animal. Do not worry if strictly speaking this is not anatomically possible. If you are going to dance, you'll fit together somehow. Spreading fingers become soaring feathers. The neat lines of human arms and legs develop the bulky shadows of a bear, or fill the round shape of a tortoise. Feet rising onto their balls become furred paws. Crooked arms reflect the eight thorn limbs of a dancing spider or, folding, adopt the precision of a mantis.

I find that my back and head are the key points. When I feel my spine curve to match the line of symmetry of my animal partner, the dance will follow. Head movements are good indicators - when I feel that I am no longer looking around as a human should, I know the dance is there.

step back at some point and watch other dancers, see the shoulder-hunch and head-drop of a big cat, or the sharp strutting curiosity of a chicken.

The degree of identification is very personal. You may enjoy a dance with the vaguest ghost of an animal wafting around your fingertips or you may submerge yourself profoundly in the furry bits. Neither is necessarily "better" or "more advanced" than the other - they offer different experiences.

This is not possession and the loss of your own identity. In all this you retain your sense of self. It is a joint venture, a sharing. There is usually a small sensible corner of your mind trying really hard not to stare but ready to kick in and bring the whole thing to a shuddering halt if it all gets too close to your more sensitive areas. This is not always helpful but you keep that "let out" clause at all times, and should be able to stop, step back and earth yourself whenever you wish. Dance on your edges but do not expect everything, or even anything, to happen all at once.

And then dance.

The dance may go anywhere. It is difficult to predict where the combination of human, animal and music will lead the dance. Out of doors, often you start by exploring the space you are in and then dancing into a story beyond it. Indoors, the music tends to set the atmosphere much more strongly.

Most people find themselves exploring the animal's natural habitat and then a story developing from that - a movement through that animal's annual cycle, or one moment of it - a migration, a hunt, who knows. The story that unfolds will be different on every occasion.

Where you have set up a more formal dance ceremony, you may set out to dance through a situation or a problem - dance your way down a storyline until you find a solution.

Go on to work with longer pieces of music and take Becoming the animal onto new depths as you dance for longer periods and move more and more freely in an Otherworld of human and animal spirit combined: dance the Great Dance and feel the vibrancy of all life that crawled from the oceans, that now flies, or is rooted in the earth, or still swims in the seas.

Going still further, we may eventually find ourselves dancing the Dream, moving into a complex where flesh, spirit and the unfolding patterns of the land itself all shape the dance.

The Circle

Action

Here is the wheel of determination that carries the journey, and is supported by it. Magic needs action, the gods appreciate effort, be prepared to step out of the temple of your head and into the world of being and doing.

We can all be warriors.

13

Becoming Active

What I know I can, I do
If think I might, I'll try
If I have only dreamed, I'll aim for it! [7]

All this book has been about contact, relationships, new friendships, new ways of meeting the world we all live in and, hopefully, discovering new avenues of wonder to explore. But it should also be about action.

Magic that remains "within" should always be questioned. If all that you have pursued here stays within the bounds of head, temple, spare bedroom or journal, then perhaps you should be asking why you have walked this trail at all.

Working animal spirits will draw you into their world, both "over there" and "over here". To see what we humans, in the "developed" societies are doing to this world "over here" and not be inspired to act on behalf of the Otherworld would seem to me to question all else that we have done.

If we are becoming "a conscious part of the endless, spreading web of connections that links everything" (from **Hop, Crawl, Slither, Fly and Swim**), not to move within that awareness is almost impossible. And "move" means just that - to be active, to work, inspired by the

Otherworld, in both the magical and "everyday" aspects of your life. Magic that remains disconnected from physical activity can seem unrooted, without substance, pointless. To simply "do" is as much a magical act as to perform the most elegant of rituals: action inspired by spirit, and conducted with awareness and clear intention can make the grubbiest and apparently mundane of tasks its own magical act.

All of this is true in much wider contexts than just "animal" ones, but in this situation see that as the challenge: finding actions within your everyday life that reflect your growing understanding of and become a strength and support for the animals you meet in the Otherworld.

We need to plan actions that we can carry through: that triad above is a guide: we need to find things that we know we can do, others that we can try to do and still others that we can aim for and eventually achieve. This is not to say that everyone should at once become vegetarian, vegan, wholly carnivorous, radically environmentalist or whatever: be realistic and find ways of accommodating change and action within your own lifestyle. At the same time, you need to be aware, once more, of your own boundaries: identifying those things that, for whatever reason, you feel you could not possibly do and then find ways to challenge those boundaries.

Yet again, you could see cycles in action:

    write a letter

    then, build a nest box

    then plant some trees

    then, help at a rescue

then, go on an expedition

then, give a talk

then, write another letter...

The details of possible actions you could take are endless and it is almost futile to start listing options but perhaps identifying areas to think about would help.

1) Start where you are: your own back yard, be it garden, yard, window box or patch of rough ground: plant flowers that feed, create a mini-pond in an old bowl, pile small pipes for ladybirds and beetles. Find ways of offering physical support to local animals: offer a refuge free of chemicals and full of food.

2) Quietly support: join a relevant society, not to be an "activist" but to give their cause the support of your money and to learn more yourself. There are specialist societies you could track down - a selection are contained in **Appendix 2**.

3) Some active support: where there is a local branch of the group you have joined, offer volunteer help: in the office, at a flag day, stuffing leaflets into envelopes at home, with jars of your exquisite peanut-butter and banana chutney. You do not have to be an expert to make a valuable contribution: all sorts of help may be needed: offer who you are. And if there is no local branch of your obscure society either start one or help someone else!

4) Get out and about: feeling fit, feet in wellies, help drag dripping things from an overgrown pond. Join a local practical conservation volunteer group and even if you are not up to digging big holes and the like there may be a gentler butterfly, bird or slug census you could help with. Get out there and "do" - and maybe you will start seeing more animals while you are about it.

5) Take a still wider view: and join in with a bigger campaign, wave a small flag, collect signatures, raise funds, wave a bigger flag.

6) Throw yourself in there, and stand among the many who are ready to face down the beaters and breakers of this world. "Non-violent direct action" is not the province of strange hairy extremists and subversives as some media would have us believe: its strength lies in all the "ordinary" people who are prepared to stand up and say "No".

It may be frightening, with thoughts of the Criminal Justice Act, aggravated trespass and social scorn hovering around. You may be about to step over the boundary of "acceptable behaviour" that you have lived with all your life.

So touch your stillness and if you feel you must go, then go as a warrior, prepared to act, inspired by spirit and walking with grace, dancing in beauty and moving from stillness. Also, take a friend, do not carry valuables but do take some form of ID, water to drink and munchies to eat and a notebook to record what happens.

Avoid trance dance and **Breath of the Beast** that might have you gnawing the legs off security guards.

Perhaps these ideas might spark your own: explore and act. If the spirits you work with are not those of local animals whose lives you can see ready support for, you might still find societies and campaigns you could support. Remember that every action helps: work here, at home, to change the world you live in and add another

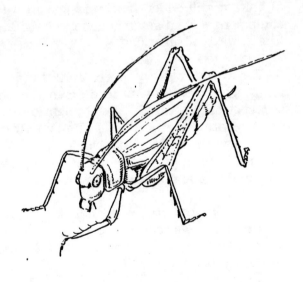

ripple of change to the wider system even if you cannot directly get out there to help your particular friends.

You might also look at the effort that is most appropriate to your relationship with spirits. If, for example, you relate directly to individual spirits (eg "fox" rather than "FOX" from **Asking Permission**) then adoption schemes and other work targeted at individual animals may feel most suitable to you while Fox and FOX people might feel happier with a group working on wider habitat and whole species issues. The difference might be that between an "adopt a whale" scheme and a "save the whales" campaign: they both work towards conservation ends but with different techniques.

We need to find our own ways of acting and to work towards the limits of those. We need to take pride in the fact that we will act, and are acting, and not be dismayed by people who seem to do so much more than us: they may not have families to raise as well, they may not have full time jobs, or whatever.

We are all needed: the battle that is engaged now, the need to protect the richness of that growing, spreading vibrant web depends as much upon the diversity of its warriors as upon their extremism. We need people working all over the place, recognising that the teacher who creates a caring, supportive growing environment for her pupils, the parent who helps his children see the world and enjoy it, the old age pensioner who keeps a bumble-bee-friendly back yard in a grim inner city area are all as important as the person lying down beneath the bull-dozer.

Change may come with devastation or through dramatic political transformation or it may come from the gradual change of more and more hearts from quiescence to determination and a readiness to act in any way they can to bring a growing and the green back into the hearts of city and people. There are no specifications on age, sex or physical ability: to be a warrior calls for the strength and stillness that comes from within. Engage heart, mind and spirit and we can all be warriors.

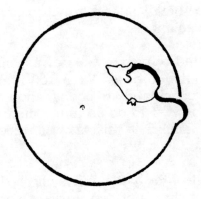

14

Touching the Dream

The opening of **Becoming Active** might be challenged:

"Magic that remains "within" should always be questioned. If all that you have pursued here stays within the bounds of head, temple, spare bedroom or journal, then perhaps you should be asking why you have walked this trail at all."

There is an argument that says magic will stand alone: that ritual has its own strength and an action performed in a magical space needs no other physical work to support it. A spoken word, a dance, a ceremony are all ways of giving shape to a dream - be it the dream of an individual or the long, slow Dream of the land. To shape a dream is enough. That action empowers the idea and its completion becomes inevitable.

This is true and for work that centres upon ourselves and our immediate concerns it does often prove to be the case. In other places, among other peoples, to dance the dance of your totem is to empower that animal or plant and your ceremonial observance is an important part of that species' energy. This usually ties in with a much closer physical bond between people and environment than we experience. Such people are not involved in conservation projects because their whole way of life belongs within their environment. They are not "outsiders" trying to get back "in" - they are "insiders" who never left.

But in the work we are covering here, we are reaching beyond human confines and touching upon the wider world. I feel that few of us here and now in our society carry such a weight of wisdom and lightness of awareness that our spells, supported by a lifetime of understanding and a culture of contact, give such substance to the magic that we can rest upon our rituals.

So now, when I meet someone who claims that he has no need to dig ponds, write a letter or plant a butterfly-friendly window-box because his magic is strong enough to change things by itself, I find myself wondering about his commitment, his arrogance and his downright laziness.

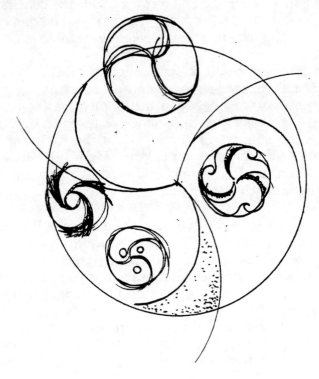

Action in both physical and non-physical worlds support each other. One gives magic shape and substance to work through while the other inspires the mundance with awareness and the celebration of something wider.

Sacred Animals is a book of a journey - a journey, hopefully, of transformation and joy, that once begun never really ends. At times in our travels we may take new routes, move into new areas or cross thresholds marked by initiation, vision, or nothing at all until we find that the world around us is not quite all it was a while before.

Somewhere along the river of your journey, you may find the current changes. One of those initiatory thresholds is met and crossed when your spirit people come to you and seek ceremony, offering you the fusion of human and animal that brings strength to both sides of the totem bond.

New ceremonies are slowly coming out of the Otherworld as relationships grow afresh and new dances chart the lfe cycles of toads and crows and tigers. These are events that mark all sorts of bonds. For the individual, it marks connections between you and your spirit companions that will last over the years, growing stronger with the repeating cycle of the ceremonies.

For groups, whether you work together regularly or meet only at those points of your personal calendars, it speaks of new identities growing where the Cat Tribe or the Wolf People share a common experience and a common connection that supports them and can reach across the divisions of race, class, sex or whatever other walls we raise. And in the Dream, it means that humans are beginning to listen. We begin the long walk home.

A ceremonial cycle is something that should not be embarked upon as some sort of pre-planned operation. When you are ready, the first movements will come to you. Maybe a single ceremony will suggest itself: "fledgeling crows" perhaps, or "strength in migration". This will probably be a ceremony to mark a dangerpoint in a species lifecycle: offering a "boost" at a critical time - a support that may be both magical and physical, as in the examples below. At first you may only act in this way once a year, the rest of the time walking more intimate paths with your companions. But the repetition is important: impetus grows slowly and over generations. Have patience, feel the changes within yourself and within your relationships and trust in the long-term pattern.

A Toad Year of ceremonies might help as an example:

Spring

ceremony: the journey to the breeding ponds.

life cycle: waking from hibernation, mass migration to spawning pools, often large casualties crossing roads.

action: helping out on "toad crossings" on recognised migration routes.

Summer

ceremony: leaving the pond - the hunt for food.

life cycle: newly metamorphosed toadlets, leave ponds for life on land.

action: interrupt grass cutting and intensive gardening wherever possible, to protect from blades and disturbance.

Autumn

ceremony: dreaming through winter - support for all toads in finding good hibernation sites and deep dreaming through the cold months

life cycle: preparation for hibernation, need for final feeding before this and to find safe sites

action: set up log or stone piles in sheltered places with lots of small crevices, keep undisturbed through the winter

"Emergency" situations may bring in other events: long dry summers may have me watering sites and performing "food finding and fat toad" ceremonies.

At other times, other animals may come to you and ask for your support. Strangers to your usual working, this may be a sign of your wider recognition and acceptance by the spirit world around you. A course of action needs to be thought through here - be humble, listen to the spirits and see what other information you can find in the everyday world.

The need of a particular animal may be met more easily through a change in physical rather than magical action. To ease a concern you may need to ask the local council to stop cutting here or burning there or draw attention to something else that is happening.

You do not necessarily have to stand there being peculiar and magical and rambling about spirits to do this: check out your facts and the place and the chances are that you can take what others may see as a "real concern" to them about animals or a habitat at risk. You may even find that you will need to go back to the spirits and explain what these people are doing and why and that if they can rest through this, next spring the bushes will be back.

Other situations may be more difficult: fox or badger digging or lamping across fields (hunting after dark with strong lights to pin-point hares with dogs to run them down), for example, are dangerous situations and you should not get into confrontation. Here combine ceremonies of strength, speed of foot, concealment and frustration of intention, with talking to local police (ask for the Wildlife Liaison Officer if they have one), countryside rangers and the local wildlife trust and offering what help you can.

At the core of this Sacred Animal journey is stepping beyond the familiar human-centred world we are used to and into a wider, wilder, more wondrous one. Here is a thought:

> *Every atom in this body existed before organic life emerged 4000 million years ago. Remember our childhood as minerals, as lava, as rocks? Rocks contain the potentiality to weave themselves into such stuff as this. We are the rocks dancing. Why do we look down on them with such a condescending air? It is they that are the immortal part of us.* [8]

We tend to live in a world where humans are seen as "top", where an, often unconscious, arrogance claims that humans are the summit of evolution: we are the end point, the ultimate achievement of the life of this planet. This may award us ownership of Earth, or maybe "stewardship" in more politically correct circles. Or we may see ourselves as the consciousness of the planet and consequently the only ones with a say in its future. However we phrase it, that arrogance gives us excuses for claiming the right to make the choices about what happens to everything else.

Yes, it is true that we can do things that no other species can. Yes, we are amazing communicators, builders, destroyers, devourers. Yes, we offer dance and music and song to the spirits, we give moving shape to a dancing magic. Yes. Yes. Yes. That makes us different. Not better. Not more important. We cannot fly as a bumble-bee does. Nothing else can. Nor do we swim like dolphins, nor cross sand with the grace of a side-winder.

So are we successful? What is success on a planetary scale? We may think of ourselves as successful and the dinosaurs as evolutionary dead-ends, long since wiped off the surface of the planet. But that lineage dominated the world for hundreds of millions of years while as human-oids we have seen a scant handful of millions. And all this stretch of time is nothing in the face of a mountain and a lifetime of growing, eroding and changing, a lifetime that sees species come and go as passing thoughts in its sleep.

There is a huge richness in diversity that is really the success of evolution, or creation, that we should celebrate. A diversity that changes, lives, dies, moves on, always becoming something more. We cannot predict the outcomes of evolutionary patterns, we can only be where we are now: living, dying, killing and being killed like everything else.

We will be swept along just like everything else. But we have the power to break the richness: to batter it back towards a simpler, less diverse world and that is what we are doing now. "Every species death diminishes me". For me, that is one of the few true sacrileges: to assume the right to remove whole species from the pattern, to move blindly and selfishly against the whole. We do not even move with clear intention, we blunder about like tantrums in a sweet shop, picking things up, dropping them, crushing them underfoot, all unseeing, and reaching out for the next morsel before we have even tasted what is already in our hands.

Willful fools: idiots and not sacred clowns, we are lining ourselves up for the remorseless hand of evolution to wipe us away when the world's systems become too frail for our constant attrition and we unleash the disease, plague, weather change that shatters us at last. In the long run of geological timescales we probably do not matter at all, life will go on, the richness diminished, but in the wake of our passing, life will go on and a new breed of dandelion will eventually lift its tufted head above the rubble. But we are animals and live and work within ecological lifetimes, and here we must be aware, here we must act.

Reach back to the celebration and maybe that should turn our arrogance towards humility that reveals us as servants of the whole web of relationship. Not servants working toward human ends at the expense of all others but as agents of change who act within the flow of the pattern. We are far from there yet: we may not get there at all but better to start walking down that path and to try than to wallow in our usual human conceits.

What is The Dream?

Throughout *Sacred Animals* I have talked about dreams and The Dream. This comes from my shamanic worldview where the only reality is in the Otherworld - in the world of dreams, if you like. The Otherworld is what lasts, changing long and slowly over the centuries while our lives and environments come and go like flickers. The physical world is the transient one, the physical world is the illusion, only the Otherworld persists. The physical world is the shape the Otherworld takes at this time. My body is a reflection of my spirit, what it is trying to be and the interaction between that and the rest of the physical world. The physical world is made up of many spirits dreaming shapes to live in.

Most of us live in our own little worlds, our own dreams, overlapping and sharing with others to a greater or lesser extent. Working through Sacred Animals you will have touched upon the "dreams" of many other spirits and hopefully will be working with a personal dream that touches harmoniously with those of a much wider range of living things. Harmony comes as we move together within the greater Dream. And that Dream may be the dream of the land, the shapes of hill, valley and river, the dynamics of energy flow through ecosystems, taking shape all the time around us.

The Dream of the land is the one that would shape our physical environment if we were not always interrupting it with our pollution and destruction. It is long and slow. To enter the Dream is to be able to walk again in old oak forest and watch the bears and wolves and even older animals that have long since gone from these hills. And beyond that is the Dream that is the universe unfolding: as I said at the beginning it may be the Hand of God, evolution, the Old Gods or the endless interactions and awareness of the spirits that makes the universe an ongoing, living, growing whole. It may be all of these. It is the Dream. Its touch is revelation, and it feels almost impossible to describe.

160

"The Tao that can be describd in words is not the true Tao"[9]

But the Dream that touches you is celebration and joy and richness beyond measure. We are all warriors: in our own unique and personal ways, we can all work for the world we live in. A warrior does not necessarily pick up a weapon to hit people with. A warrior may be the one who is prepared to stand first and say "no" - or say "yes" and lead the celebration. A warrior has the courage to act on the moment, action balanced by a longer, wider, deeper awareness that inspires the thought and the moment. Whatever you can do, do, act with grace and joy and strength and trust. We can all be warriors.

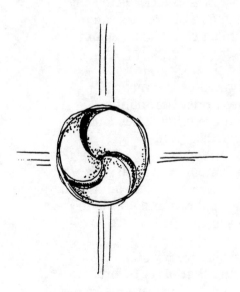

Appendix 1: The Fabled Hare

Taken from the album *"Year"* by Maddy Prior (PRKCD20) on Park Records, PO Box 651, Oxford, OX2 9AZ

I sall goe until a hare
I sall goe until a hare
Wi sorrow and sick mickle care
I sall goe in the devil's name
An while I come home again.

Ruled by the moon
I am ruled by the moon
I move under her mantle
I am the symbol of her moods
Of rebirth's cycle

I am companion to the gods
I can conceive while I am pregnant
I call the dawn and spring in
I am the advent

I bring life from water
In a cup that must be broken
I whisper to the bursting egg
I'm Aestre's token

Scent of Dog
Scent of dog
  Scent of man

Closer closer smell them coming
Hot breath
  Hot death
Closer closer hard the running.

Tongues pant
  Hearts thump
Closer closer through the fields
Teeth snap
  Bones crack
Closer closer at my heels.

Nearer yet and nearer
  I can feel the poacher's knife
He is running for his dinner
  I am running for my life.

Winter Wakeneth

Winter wakeneth al my care,
nou this leues waxeth bare;
ofte y sike ant mourne sare
  when hit cometh in my thoht
  of this worldes joie hou hit geth al to noht.

The Hare Said

Man sprays no weeds
  The scythe cuts the corn bleeds
Leverets trapped in a harvest blade
  Tis the time of man the hare said.

Here's the tractor here's the plough
  And where shall we go now
We'll lie in forms as still as the dead
  In the open fields the hare said.

No cover but the camouflage
  From the winter's wild and bitter rage

All our defense is in our legs
We run like the wind the hare said.

I shall run and run
I've been cursed I've been despised
as a witch with darkest powers
- I sall goe until a hare -
I've been hunted, trapped and punished
in these my darkest hours
- wi sorrow and such mickle care -

I've been thrown into the fire
but I do not fear it
It purifies and resurrects
and I can bear it

I have outrun dogs and foxes
and I've dodged your tractor wheels
I've survived your persecution
and your ever-changing fields

I will run and run forever
where the wild fields are mine
I'm a symbol of endurance
running through the mists of time

Appendix 2: Organisations

This list cannot even pretend to be comprehensive but offers a selection of environmental organisations which you might choose to support. In this list I have tried to find organisations with animal related campaigns rather than those that might work more on plant or land human population, environmental development and econonmic issues. Inclusion in this list does not mean that I know, have worked with or necessarily endorse the stance that these groups might take. When writing for information, it helps to include a large SAE.

International Campaigning Groups

Environmental Investigation Agency, 15 Bowling Green
     Lane, London, EC1R 0BD
Friends of the Earth, 26 - 28 Underwood Street, London,
     N1 7JQ
Greenpeace, 30 -31 Islington Green, London, N1 8XE

People's Trust for Endangered Species, Hamble House,
    Meadrow, Godalming, Surrey, GU7 3JX
Rainforest Foundation, 37 Great Guildford Street,
    London, SE1 0ES
Women's Environment Network, 22 Highbury Grove,
    London, N5 2EA
World Society for the Protection of Animals (WSPA), 2
    Langley Lane, London SW8 1TJ
Worldwide Land Conservation Trust (or World Land Trust),
    Blyth House, Bridge Street, Halesworth, Suffolk,
    IP19 8AB - runs projects buying and managing
    land in belize, Costa Rica and the Philippines
Worldwide Fund for Nature (WWF), Panda House, Weyside
    Park, Catteshall lane, Godalming, Surrey, GU7 1XR

National Organisations

British Trust for Conservation Volunteers, 36 St Mary's
    Street, Wallingford, Oxfordshire, OX10 0EJ - local
    groups and regional offices organise practical work
    all over the country
Mammal Society, 15 Cloisters Business House, 8
    Battersea Park Road, London, SW8 4BG - all
    aspects of British mammals
Marine Conservation Society, 9 Gloucester Road, Ross-on-
    Wye, Herefordshire, HR9 5BU - British coastal
    conservation

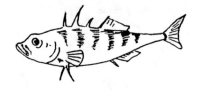

Royal Society for Nature Conservation (RSNC), The Green,
Nettleham Lincolnshire, LN2 2NR - contact point
for the County, and some Urban, Wildlife Trusts -
local reserves, issues and national campaigns.
This address is also the headquarters for WATCH, a
large conservation organisation for young people
Royal Society for the Prevention of Cruelty to Animals
Headquarters (RSPCA), Causeway, Horsham, West
Sussex, RH12 1HG Britain's leading animal welfare
organisation - regional and local offices in
telephone book
Royal Society for the Protection of Birds (RSPB), The
Lodge, Sandy, Bedfordshire, SG19 2DL - also the
base for the Young Ornithologists' Club
Wildfowl & Wetlands Trust, Slimbridge, Gloucestershire,
GL2 7BT

Local Contacts

There may well be local branches of your county or urban
wildlife trust (contact RSNC above) or of some of the other
societies listed above and below. Good starting points for
information, as well as local libraries, are countryside and
urban ranger and warden services. Their Visitor Centres
are often informal meeting points for interested people and
the service itself may well run volunteer groups and public
events programmes offering all sorts of activities.

Specific Groups of Animals

Bat Groups of Great Britain, 15 Cloisters Business House,
8 Battersea Park Road, London, SW8 4BG
British Butterfly Conservation Society, Tudor House, 102
Chaveney Road, Quorn, Leicester, LE12 8AD

British Herpetological Society, c/o Zoological Society of
London, Regents Park, London, NW1 4RY
Care for the Wild, 1 Ashfolds, Horsham Road, Rusper, W
Sussex, RH12 4QX (chimpanzee campaign among
others)
Cheetalert, The Lifeline Survival Trust, Grassendale,
Woodcombe, Minehead, Somerset, TA24 8SB -
conservation of cheetahs
The Dian Fossey Gorilla Fund UK, 110 Gloucester Ave,
London, NW1 8JA - raises money to ensure the 650
mountain gorillas left in the world survive
The Hawk & Owl Trust, 15 Butterfield Road,
Wheathamstead, Herts, AL4 8PX
International Otter Survival Fund, Broadford, Isle of Skye,
IV49 9AQ
International Wildlife Coalition Trust (Whale Adopt), Dept
96, BBC3, PO Box 73, Hartfield, East Sussex, TN7
4EY run a Humpback Whale adoption scheme
Libearty: work to protect bears - contact through WSPA,
address above
National Federation of Badger Groups, 15 Cloisters
Business House, 8 Battersea Park Road, London,
SW8 4BG
Orang-utan Foundation, 7 Kent Terrace, London NW1 4RP
Rare Breeds Survival Trust, RBST Freepost (WLM),
National Agricultural Centre, Kenilworth, Coventry, CV8
2BR - support 49 endangered British breeds of
cattle, sheep, pigs, horses, ponies and goats
The Tiger Trust, Chevington, Bury St Edmunds, Suffolk,
IP29 5RG
World Parrot Trust, Glanmer House, Hayle, Cornwall,
TR27 4HY
Whale & Dolphin Conservation Society, Freepost (SN863),
Bath, BA1 2XF
Wolf Society of Great Britain, Prospect House, Charlton,
Kilmersdon, Bath, BA3 5TN
Wolfwatch, 5 Delapre Drive, Banbury, Oxon, OX16 7WP

References

1. Maddy Prior, The Fabled Hare, taken from the album "Year" (PRKCD20) on Park records
2. Maddy Prior, as above
3. Maddy Prior, as above
4. Gordon MacLellan, personal journal
5. Scriver, Bob: The Blackfeet, artists of the Northern Plains, The Lowell Press, 1990
6. Verne Dusenberry, quoted in Brown, J. E.: Animals of the Soul, Element, 1992
7. Gordon MacLellan, personal journal
8. John Seed, from "We are the rocks dancing" in Seed J. et al: Thinking Like A Mountain, Heretic Books, 1988
9. Lao Tzu: The Tao Te Ching

Bibliography

A selection books I know and enjoy and would recommend which you can cheerfully ignore and go off and find your own. I gave up trying to be inclusive - folktale collections, for example, could run on indefinitely. Approach this list as possible starting points for your own reading and certainly do not view it in any way as exclusive!

A core group (try some of these even if none of the others)

Attenborough, David:The Living Planet, Collins, 1984 - also look out for Life on Earth and The Trials of Life

BBC Wildlife Magazine: monthly, in newsagents: invaluable up to date information and articles

Durrell, Gerald: My Family and Other Animals, Rupert Hart-Davis, 1958 - and all the others since!

Franklin, Anna: Familiars - Animal Powers of Britain, Capall Bann 1997

Hoban, Russell & Gentleman, David: The Dancing Tigers, Jonathon Cape, 1993

MacLellan, Gordon: Talking to the Earth: environmental art activities, Capall Bann, 1995

various authors: Collins Field Guides - to a wide range of groups of animals and plants

various authors: Whittet World Wildlife and British Natural History series, examples: Peter Shirley Urban Wildlife, Michael Chinery: Garden Creepy-crawlies, Pat Morris: Hedgehogs

Wyatt, Gary: Spirit Faces, Thames & Hudson, 1994

Natural history

Bouchner, Miroslav: Animal Tracks and Traces, Octopus, 1982
Brown, Roy, et al: Tracks and Signs of the Birds of Britain and Europe, Helm 1987
Corbet, G.B. & Harris, S: The Handbook of British Mammals, Blackwell, 1991
King, Angela & Clifford, Sue: Holding Your Ground, Maurice Temple Smith, 1985
Macdonald, David: The Velvet Claw, BBC Books, 1992
Rackham, Oliver: History of the Countryside, George Weidenfeld and Nicolson, Ltd, 1986

Stories, mythologies and poems

Caduto, M. J. & Bruchac, J: Keepers of the Animals, Fulcrum, 1991
Hughes, Ted: Tales of the Early World, Faber & Faber, 1988
Napaljarri and Cataldi: Warlpirri Dreamings and Histories, Harper Collins, 1994
Sheldon, Dyan & Blythe, Gary: The Whales' Song, Red Fox, 1993

Making things

Coult, Tony & Kershaw, Baz: Engineers of the Imagination, Methuen, 1983
Evans, Judy & Powell, Hazel: Inspirations for Dance and Movement, Scholastic 1994
Hoggett, Charles: Stage Crafts, Black, 1975
Hunt, W Ben: The Complete How-to Book of Indiancraft, Collier Macmillan, 1973

Petrash, Carol: Earthwise: environmental crafts and activities with young children, Floris 1992

Reference, Inspiration and Other People's Ideas

Aburrow, Yvonne: Auguries and Omens - The Magical Lore of Birds, Capall Bann 1994

Andrews, Ted: Animal-speak, Llewellyn, 1995

Brown, Joseph Epes: Animals of the Soul, Element, 1992

Campbell, Joseph: Historical Atlas of World Mythology Vol 1: The Way of the Animal Powers, part 1: mythologies of the primitive hunters and gatherers and part 2: mythologies of the great hunt, Harper & Row, 1988

Cornell, Joseph: Listening to Nature, Exley, 1987 Sharing Nature with Children, Exley

Davies, Marion: Magical Lore of Cats, Capall Bann 1996

Davies, Marion: Lore of the Sacred Horse, Capall Bann, 1995

Green, Miranda: Animals in Celtic Life and Myth, Routledge, 1992

Herold, Erich: The World of Masks, Hamlyn, 1992

Heth, Charlotte: Native American Dance: ceremonies and social traditions, Fulcrum/Smithsonian 1993

Lister, Margot: Costume, Barrie & Jenkins, 1967

Lonsdale, Steven: Animals and the Origins of Dance, Thames & Hudson 1981

Mails, Thomas E.: The Mystic Warriors of the Plains, Aurum Press, 1995

McQuiston, et al: In The Spirit Of Mother Earth, Chronicle, 1994

Rockwell, David: Giving Voice to Bear, Roberts Rinehart, 1991

Roth, Gabrielle: Maps to Ecstasy, Crucible, 1990

Scriver, Bob: The Blackfeet, artists of the Northern Plains,
   The Lowell Press, 1990
Tilke, Max: Costume Patterns and Designs, Magna, 1990

FREE DETAILED CATALOGUE

A detailed illustrated catalogue is available on request, SAE or International Postal Coupon appreciated. Titles are available direct from Capall Bann, post free in the UK (cheque or PO with order) or from good bookshops and specialist outlets. Title currently available include:

Animals, Mind Body Spirit & Folklore
Angels and Goddesses - Celtic Christianity & Paganism by Michael Howard
Arthur - The Legend Unveiled by C Johnson & E Lung
Auguries and Omens - The Magical Lore of Birds by Yvonne Aburrow
Book of the Veil The by Peter Paddon
Call of the Horned Piper by Nigel Jackson
Cats' Company by Ann Walker
Celtic Lore & Druidic Ritual by Rhiannon Ryall
Compleat Vampyre - The Vampyre Shaman: Werewolves & Witchery by Nigel Jackson
Crystal Clear - A Guide to Quartz Crystal by Jennifer Dent
Earth Dance - A Year of Pagan Rituals by Jan Brodie

Earth Magic by Margaret McArthur
Enchanted Forest - The Magical Lore of Trees by Yvonne Aburrow
Healing Homes by Jennifer Dent
Herbcraft - Shamanic & Ritual Use of Herbs by Susan Lavender & Anna Franklin
In Search of Herne the Hunter by Eric Fitch
Inner Space Workbook - Developing Counselling & Magical Skills Through the Tarot
Kecks, Keddles & Kesh by Michael Bayley
Living Tarot by Ann Walker
Magical Incenses and Perfumes by Jan Brodie
Magical Lore of Animals by Yvonne Aburrow
Magical Lore of Cats by Marion Davies

Magical Lore of Herbs by Marion Davies
Masks of Misrule - The Horned God & His Cult in Europe by Nigel Jackson
Mysteries of the Runes by Michael Howard
Oracle of Geomancy by Nigel Pennick
Patchwork of Magic by Julia Day
Pathworking - A Practical Book of Guided Meditations by Pete Jennings
Pickingill Papers - The Origins of Gardnerian Wicca by Michael Howard
Psychic Animals by Dennis Bardens
Psychic Self Defence - Real Solutions by Jan Brodie
Runic Astrology by Nigel Pennick
Sacred Animals by Gordon MacLellan
Sacred Grove - The Mysteries of the Forest by Yvonne Aburrow
Sacred Geometry   by Nigel Pennick
Sacred Lore of Horses The by Marion Davies
Sacred Ring - Pagan Origins British Folk Festivals & Customs by Michael Howard
Secret Places of the Goddess by Philip Heselton
Talking to the Earth by Gordon Maclellan
Taming the Wolf - Full Moon Meditations by Steve Hounsome
The Goddess Year by Nigel Pennick & Helen Field
West Country Wicca by Rhiannon Ryall
Witches of Oz The by Matthew & Julia Phillips

Capall Bann is owned and run by people actively involved in many of the areas in which we publish. Our list is expanding rapidly so do contact us for details on the latest releases. We guarantee our mailing list will never be released to other companies or organisations.

Capall Bann Publishing, Freshfields, Chieveley, Berks, RG20 8TF